MOHAMMED, CHARLEMAGNE & THE ORIGINS OF EUROPE

Archaeology and the Pirenne Thesis

Richard Hodges &
David Whitehouse

trade persisted, but rather it was the fall of the A-C. in 790, affecting which affected int'l trade greatly, that the middle ages began.

Cornell University Press
Ithaca, New York

First published 1983 by Cornell University Press.
First printing, Cornell Paperbacks, 1983.
Fifth printing 1996.

International Standard Book Number (cloth) 0-8014-1615-9
International Standard Book Number (paper) 0-8014-9262-9
Library of Congress Catalog Card Number 82-74020
Printed in the United States of America

⊚The paper in this book meets the minimum requirements of the
American National Standard for Information Sciences—Permanence
of Paper for Printed Library Materials, ANSI Z39.48-1984.

Contents

To Klavs Randsborg

Preface

In medieval history it is no longer the fashion to tackle major issues, and most historians are engaged in detailed descriptions of the trees rather than in an analysis of the wood as a whole. All too often, general or 'popular' histories are dull and uncontroversial. We have come a long way from the vulgarising histories, to borrow a phrase from Ferdinand Lot, of Lot himself or Henri Pirenne, and a long way too from the general histories of their most brilliant pupils, Braudel, Bloch and Duby. At the beginning of the century, many documents of fundamental importance had only just become available in critical editions, providing the stimulus for a reappraisal of earlier accounts. Another equally important flood of information is becoming available today, and historians face the exciting prospect of another change of perspective.

The new data come not from manuscripts, but from archaeological research. Although medievalists have employed archaeology for over a century, they have tended to use it simply to illustrate conclusions drawn from the documents, rather than to open a dialogue between students of material culture and of the written word.

But times are changing. The archaeology of the period A.D. 500-1000 has taken off in the Mediterranean (where prehistoric and classical studies formerly enjoyed a virtual monopoly in most areas) and in the Islamic world. Here, as in northern Europe, field survey, careful excavation and improved methods of dating are beginning to supply information which now is not only more abundant but also of much higher quality than ever before. The 'New Archaeology', pioneered in the United States in the 1960s, has taught the archaeologist the value of anthropological models in the study of the past. The new data and models positively compel us to take a new look at the written sources and reconsider the 'making of the Middle Ages'.

This short book attempts to prove the point. *Mohammed and Charlemagne*, Pirenne's classic history of Europe between the fifth and ninth centuries, although nearly fifty years old, is still an important work.[1] Many parts of its bold framework have been attacked, but seldom decisively, for until now the evidence has been insufficient. In the following pages we shall review the 'Pirenne thesis' in the light of archaeological information from northern Europe, the Mediterranean and western Asia. We have two objectives: to tackle the major issue of the origins of the Carolingian Empire and to indicate the almost staggering potential of the archaeological data.

This book, then, is an attempt to rekindle interest in an important set of questions and to draw attention to new sets of data. Fresh evidence will eventually resolve many of our present uncertainties, and we have no illusions that the explanations we offer are in any way permanent. Indeed, we shall be more than content if we succeed only in persuading readers to look across traditional boundaries between classical and medieval, east and west, history and archaeology. In the words of Pirenne's biographer, we would like to recapture 'the timeless vibrance of his history'.

The book developed from conversations between us when Richard Hodges held a Leverhulme European Research Fellowship at the British School at Rome in 1980. It will be apparent, however, that we have also gained much from our recent and current excavations, the results of which have been woven into the themes treated here. Richard Hodges thanks his colleagues who took part in the San Vincenzo Project, especially Amanda Claridge, Peter Hayes, John Mitchell and Chris Wickham, who have discussed many questions underlying the Pirenne thesis. He is also grateful to Kirsten Bendixen, Philip Grierson, Henry Hurst and Michael Metcalf for information, guidance and valuable conversations, and to many participants at seminars in Aarhus, Amsterdam, Bergen, Copenhagen, Durham, Lund, Oslo, Oxford and Sheffield during 1981-82. His

[1] See Peter Brown, '*Mohammed and Charlemagne* by Henri Pirenne', *Daedalus*, 103, 1974, 25-33.

greatest debt is to Klavs Randsborg, who has been an inspiring friend and has helped to clarify many murky points in the discussion.

David Whitehouse thanks the British Institute of Persian Studies, the British School at Rome and the Society for Libyan Studies, which have given him the opportunity to work in Iran, Italy and Libya. The chapters which follow contain information derived from excavations at Siraf, Iran; Anguillara Sabazia, Farfa (co-directed with Charles McClendon) and the Schola Praeconum, Italy; Ajdabiyan, Libya – to all those associated with these projects he extends his warmest thanks.

Thanks are due also to Debbie Hodges for the typing, to Jacqueline A. Nowakowski for the drawings, and to the following for photographs: Academia Belgica, Rome (Fig. 1); Graeme Barker (Figs. 16, 19); George Bass (Fig. 21); Kirsten Bendixen (Figs. 45, 68); the British Museum (Figs. 25, 38); Joseph Cloutman and the Siraf Expedition (Figs. 56 and 60); the Dutch State Archaeological Service (R.O.B.) through the kindness of W.A. van Es and Pim Verwers for Figs. 29, 37, 42, 63, 64; Prof. Dieter Eckstein (Fig. 3); Clive Foss (Fig. 20); Henry Hurst (Figs. 2, 8); Institute of Archaeology, University of London (Fig. 62); A.H.S. Megaw, Richard Anderson and Dumbarton Oaks (Fig. 22); Demetrios Michaelides (Fig. 26); John Mitchell (Fig. 70); Paolo Peduto (Fig. 12); Römisch Germanisches Zentralmuseum, Mainz (Fig. 32); Kurt Schietzel for obtaining Fig. 43 belonging to the Landesmuseum für Vor-Frühgeschichte, Schleswig; Giles Sholl and the Siraf Expedition (Figs. 50, 57, 58, 59); Statens Historiska Museum, Stockholm (Figs. 46, 47, 49); Bryan Ward-Perkins (Figs. 5, 9, 67).

Sheffield and Rome   R.H.,D.W.
May 1983

1. Mohammed, Charlemagne and Pirenne

Great historians, like all great men, cast long shadows. To some extent this is because the greatest historians are part of the history they have written, and so Herodotus, Bede, Gibbon and Carlyle are studied just as their works are studied. Few twentieth-century historians are yet eligible for these exalted ranks, though if we were required to name the foremost contender Henri Pirenne would no doubt spring immediately to mind. Pirenne was once called 'a prince in the realm of history with few equals and with none greater';[1] he has had enormous influence on the study of European medieval history and has provoked one of the most exciting debates in the field.

Pirenne was born in 1862, a son of the new state of Belgium which had recently won its liberty from the Netherlands. He was to become one of its most celebrated citizens, and by the time of his death in 1935 he was a national figure. First and foremost a historian of Belgium, as most schoolchildren of that country are well aware, his massive *Histoire de Belgique* is eloquent testimony to his intense patriotism. Pirenne was a hero, too, for he defied the German invaders during the First World War and as a result was put in a concentration camp. (The impact of his imprisonment on world opinion was such that the President of the United States and the Pope interceded with the Kaiser on his behalf, but without success.)

In his confined, but paradoxically cosmopolitan life behind barbed wire, Pirenne felt compelled to look beyond the problems of Belgian history and develop his earlier thoughts on the history and economy of post-Roman Europe. After his release in 1918 he concentrated on these broader themes, publishing a series of articles and books which are now known collectively as the 'Pirenne thesis'. They were among the first

[1] Bryce Lyon, *Henri Pirenne – a biographical and intellectual study*, Ghent 1974, 414.

Fig. 1 Commemorative medallion of Henri Pirenne. (Courtesy the Director, Academia Belgica, Rome)

attempts at economic history, diverging markedly from the narrative tradition of the nineteenth century. It is these studies that have made Pirenne eligible for a place among the immortals of historiography.[2]

In prison, Pirenne contemplated the breakdown of the classical world and the emergence of the Middle Ages. His explanation of the process was first presented in a short paper entitled 'Mahomet et Charlemagne', published in a Belgian journal in 1922, and he developed the theme in lectures to the International Historical Congress in Brussels in 1923 and in Oslo in 1928. These new ideas also formed a vital part of the early chapters of *Medieval Cities* (1925) – a book derived from

[2] Ibid.: see also S. Reynolds, *An Introduction to the History of English Medieval Towns*, Oxford 1977, 17.

lectures at Princeton which has continued to make an impression on the English-speaking world. In the 1930s he modified and substantiated many aspects of the thesis, and drafted his important book *Mohammed and Charlemagne*.[3]

The first draft was completed on 4 May 1935. Pirenne never revised it; doubtless he would have done so, but he died later that month. The manuscript was carefully corrected by his son, Count Jacques Pirenne, who with the assistance of his father's student, Ferdinand Vercauteren, saw it through the press. Though by no means a polished expression of his historical model, the book is without question a remarkably explicit statement of Pirenne's views.

The thesis was constructed against a background of intellectual stagnation in medieval history. Since the Renaissance, historians had stressed the 'Gothic' bleakness of the Dark Ages and focussed on the cataclysmic impact of Attila's Huns on the rich civilisation of Rome early in the fifth century. This, of course, was the focal point of Gibbon's monumental history, which in turn became the subject of detailed scrutiny by nineteenth-century historians. As a result, historians of the ancient world terminated their studies with the fifth century, while their medieval counterparts began with the Germanic inundation of western Europe from that time on, a schism that still to some extent remains. The 'Romanists' regard the German occupation of the Western Empire as the beginning of a dark age, while medievalists are tempted to reflect – thankfully, perhaps – on the collapse of a decadent and uncreative monster and the conception of new and vigorous political entities. Henri Pirenne was the first historian to stand back from these entrenched views of the past and to consider the interactions between the ancient and medieval worlds.

Mohammed and Charlemagne is divided into two parts, the first entitled 'Western Europe before Islam', and the second 'Islam and the Carolingians'. The first chapter argues that the migrant tribes of the fourth to sixth centuries preserved what political institutions they could and did not therefore

---

[3] Henri Pirenne, *Medieval Cities*, Princeton 1925; *Mohammed and Charlemagne*, London 1939 (translated from the 10th edition in French).

deliberately destroy classical civilisation. The second presents evidence to support the thesis, and in particular argues the case that trading relations continued within the Mediterranean. Chapter 3 shows that the Germanic invaders also made a determined effort to preserve classical culture in all its forms – a goal reinforced by the Church, which attempted to do the same. The second part of the book analyses the impact of the Islamic conquests in north Africa, the eastern Mediterranean and Spain during the seventh and early eighth centuries, concluding that the Moslems effectively overthrew 'Roman' mastery of the sea lanes and as a result were able to separate the remnants of the Western Empire from the Eastern Empire, ruled from Byzantium. The central theme of the book is that these dramatic changes in the Mediterranean isolated the Merovingian kings in north-west Europe and caused the gradual rise of the Carolingians, who were economically remote from the Mediterranean. Similarly, the isolation of Italy compelled the Pope to ally himself with the aspiring Carolingian dynasty in the later eighth century, and ultimately led to the coronation of Charlemagne as Emperor in Rome on Christmas Day, 800. Finally, the book discusses the overall implications of these events for the culture and economy of the West. The most famous passage concludes:

> It is therefore strictly correct to say that without Mohammed Charlemagne would have been inconceivable. In the seventh century the ancient Roman Empire had actually become an Empire of the East; the Empire of Charles was an Empire of the West ... The Carolingian Empire, or rather, the Empire of Charlemagne, was the scaffolding of the Middle Ages.[4]

Pirenne therefore proposed that the demise of the classical world was postponed until the seventh century. At the same time he emphasised the significance of Islamic expansion during the course of that century. He was arguing that the nexus of change lay in the brief period after about 645 when

[4] Ibid., 234-5

two hostile civilisations faced each other across the Mediterranean. Isolated in this fashion, he argued, urban life in the West collapsed and political power became focussed on land holdings. The commercial middle classes disappeared and power became concentrated in the hands of the Church. Finally, it was Charlemagne who decisively altered the situation, standing astride the gap between a static closed economy and an emergent, fluid one.

On the whole historians are wary, perhaps too wary, of broad generalising themes, but Pirenne's thesis demanded attention because he had spent a lifetime refining his argument. His brilliant generalisations have attracted an enormous volume of critical comment, both from historians and from numismatists. But archaeologists, as we shall see, have so far played only a minor part in the debate.

At first the debate was concentrated on Pirenne's interpretation of the documentary sources, and he was criticised for emphasising some points too much and others too little. For example, did the Moslems really have such a decisive impact on trade within the Mediterranean? The 'four disappearances' of papyrus, oriental luxury textiles, spices and gold currency, as Robert S. Lopez showed, 'were not contemporary either with the Arab advance or with each other'.[6] Indeed can we not detect a growing isolation of Gaul as early as the third or fourth century, two hundred years before – according to Pirenne – the change occurred. Nearly all the contributors to the debate, however, acknowledge the inadequacy of the documentary sources; the same exiguous data can be used to support sharply contrasting points of view. The crucial information presented on trade, for example, is drawn largely from a handful of saints' lives, from miscellaneous letters, and from a few legislative documents and charters. To take just one example, Gregory of Tours' *History of the Franks* is used repeatedly in Chapter 2, which discusses the economic and social circumstances of the seventh century, but how reliable is Gregory of Tours? How

[5] See Lyon, op. cit., 431ff., 461-7.

[6] Robert S. Lopez, 'Mohammed and Charlemagne: a revision', *Speculum* 18, 1943, 14-38.

familiar was he with recent events all over Europe? And was he in a position to assess the state of the Frankish economy? The documentary evidence that survives is simply inadequate to provide the answers; as a result, great importance was attached to the numismatic evidence.

Pirenne himself made some use of the coinage of the early medieval period, and often alluded to the studies of Merovingian coinage published by his friend the numismatist, Maurice Prou. His student Vercauteren and another numismatist, Gentilhomme, were soon to contribute to the debate with detailed analyses of Merovingian and Carolingian coin-hoards, which implied that coins were circulated internally on a wide scale within the Merovingian kingdom and the Empire which replaced it. Archibald Lewis has elaborated this theme, and in recent years the coin-hoards have been evaluated again to prove, it is claimed, the prosperity of north-west Europe in the eighth and ninth centuries.[7] But of all these documentary and numismatic studies, perhaps the most original have been those of Sture Bolin and Maurice Lombard, who deployed the full range of the sources to modify Pirenne's thesis and take it in new directions.

Bolin studied the Scandinavian coinage for a thesis which he submitted in the 1930s; sadly it was never published, and twenty years later a short derivative essay appeared in English under the title 'Mohammed, Charlemagne and Ruric'.[8] Bolin was the first scholar to make use of the large number of coins that had been hoarded by the Vikings in Scandinavia and Russia. He asserted 'that an examination of the hoards from Carolingian times will show fairly directly how close the connections were between the Frankish and Arab worlds … '.[9]

---

[7] These arguments are brilliantly reviewed by Philip Grierson, 'Commerce in the Dark Ages: a critique of the evidence', *Transactions of the Royal Historical Society* (5th series) 9, 1959, 123-40; see also Karl F. Morrison, 'Numismatics and Carolingian trade: a critique of the evidence', *Speculum* 38, 1963, 61-73; and D.M. Metcalf, 'The prosperity of north-western Europe in the eighth and ninth centuries', *Economic History Review* 20, 1967, 344-57.

[8] Sture Bolin, 'Mohammed, Charlemagne and Ruric', *Scandinavian Economic History Review* 1, 1952.

[9] Ibid.

In other words, Bolin set out to show that 'one may reiterate Pirenne's paradox without Mohammed, no Charlemagne, but in disagreement, not in accord with his views'. He tried to show that the design, the weight and to some extent the value of the Frankish denier was determined by contemporary Islamic silver coinage, and illustrated this close connection by a graph suggesting that Charlemagne's coin reforms were based on an Islamic model. Moreover he pointed to the clear evidence of flourishing trade in the Islamic world and around the North Sea in the Carolingian period. In a sense, he was trying to shift the focus of attention away from the heart of Europe, which had often been described, to the periphery, where abundant numismatic and archaeological evidence demanded the reinterpretation of at least one section of *Mohammed and Charlemagne*.

Lombard's thesis was founded on a belief that gold circulated continuously in the West despite poor evidence for its existence during the Dark Ages. He pointed out that at the beginning of the seventh century there were three monetary zones. The first was the West, where a passive balance of trade ultimately resulted in the drainage of its gold reserves. The second was the eastern Mediterranean, where the supply of gold had ceased but large hoards still existed in, for example, Egyptian and Syrian churches. The third lay beyond Byzantium, for the Sasanian Empire had acquired large quantities of gold in its political and economic relations with the Eastern Roman Empire but kept it out of circulation, preferring instead to use silver as a primary means of exchange. This part of Lombard's argument was essentially an elaboration of the Pirenne thesis, but he suggested next that as the Arabs advanced into the Byzantine and Sasanian empires large supplies of gold fell into their hands. There were the great churches of the eastern Mediterranean, for example, and the possibility of controlling the lucrative trade routes to Nubia and West Africa, where the principal gold mines were located. Lombard claimed that the West obtained some of this gold in return for raw materials like timber, furs, minerals and slaves, and that this commerce is reflected by the hoards and finds of Moslem dirhems in European Russia from the later eighth century onwards. It was this relationship between Islam and Europe, he maintained, that ultimately brought about the economic revival of the West.[10]

These are two of the most oustanding numismatic critiques of *Mohammed and Charlemagne* because, like Pirenne, both Bolin and Lombard tried to go beyond the limitations of the historical sources. Soon, however, their hypotheses were attacked and discarded. Lombard's argument was inherently weak because gold coins of the period are scarce, though references to gold itself are more frequent. Similarly, Bolin's arguments were attacked because Islamic dirhems are extremely scarce in western Europe, and the number of early ninth-century hoards in Scandinavia and Russia is small compared with the number dating from the tenth century. Bolin, it should be said, was well aware of the scarcity of dirhems in Carolingian contexts and attributed it to the melting down of these heretically inscribed coins once they reached Christian toll-stations. Both hypotheses can be tested, however, now that archaeologists are uncovering evidence for trade with northern Europe and we are gaining an increasingly detailed picture of commerce in the Baltic Sea during Viking times. As we shall see, archaeologists are injecting new life into the complex theories advanced by these two critics of Pirenne.

Bolin and to a lesser extent Lombard were aware of the need for new perspectives, but their economic interpretations were formed in essentially traditional moulds. This traditional approach remained intact until Philip Grierson offered a new interpretation of the economic implications of Pirenne's thesis. In his celebrated paper 'Commerce in the Dark Ages: a critique of the evidence' (1959), Grierson declared:

> All that we know of the social conditions of the time suggests that the alternatives to trade were more important than trade itself: the *onus probandi* rests on those who believe the contrary to have been the case.[11]

---

[10] Maurice Lombard, 'L'or musulman du VIIe au XIe siècles. Les bases monetaires d'une suprématie économique, *Annales ESC* 2, 1947, 143-60; 'Mahomet et Charlemagne. Le problème économique', *Annales ESC* 3, 1948, 188-99.

[11] Grierson, op. cit., 140.

In his discussion of continental trade with Middle Saxon England (between the seventh and ninth centuries), Grierson drew attention to the social importance of exchange, and in particular to 'gift exchange', a concept he derived from the works of Bronislav Malinowski and Marcel Mauss, two anthropologists who had set the study of primitive economics on a scientific basis just after the First World War.[12] The main thrust of Grierson's essay was to emphasise that by the time of the Dark Ages the social dimension of exchange was probably more important than the economic one. In other words the economic matrix was entirely different from that of the Roman period, which was based on firm market-place principles. For example, he showed that the existence of coins at this time need not be indicative of regular market-place transactions, as most historians had believed, but that they might have been minted for purely social purposes, such as the payment of blood price or even (before the arrival of Christianity) as offerings to the gods to transport the body to the afterlife.[13] Grierson's interpretation is easier to describe than to prove, simply because an Anglo-Saxon coin bears a closer resemblance to a Roman coin or to a modern penny than it does to the shells of the Trobriand Islanders which first aroused Malinowski's interest in economic anthropology. Nevertheless a more recent analysis of the Anglo-Saxon sources has confirmed the significance of gift-exchange, and as a result Grierson's study has become the object of renewed attention.[14]

Even so, one has the distinct impression that historians and numismatists have spent too long re-working the same information. Since Pirenne's conclusions are based on an interpretation of economic data, new economic information would be immensely useful. Archaeology enables us to enlarge the data base. For instance, we can find and date evidence for the

[12] Bronislav Malinowski, *Argonauts of the Western Pacific*, London 1922; Marcel Mauss, *Essai sur le don*, Paris 1925.

[13] Grierson, op. cit.

[14] See, for example, T.M. Charles-Edwards, 'The distinction between land and moveable wealth in Anglo-Saxon England', in P.H. Sawyer (ed.), *Medieval Settlement: continuity and change*, London 1976, 180-7.

decay of Roman towns. We can detect the manufacture and distribution of certain traded goods, like pottery, glassware, stone objects, jewellery and in some cases textiles. We can also detect changes in building plans, in settlement locations and in diet (by using animal bones) and discuss social and economic questions. Nevertheless it is widely held that archaeologists are simply antiquarians, who do little more than list finds and speculate upon their meaning, a deep-rooted prejudice which is only slowly giving way to respect as they produce more and more evidence for past societies. Medieval archaeology, in particular, is still in its infancy, and the discipline's necessary pre-occupation with large-scale projects in the face of destruction by redevelopment has inhibited its integration with traditional, archive-oriented 'history'. But archaeology is slowly losing its image as the simple provider of illustrative material, and a growing awareness has at last arisen among historians that it can offer concrete information and test hypotheses.

Over the last twenty years medieval archaeology has developed rapidly in order to meet the everyday threats to our heritage, but even in the 1920s there was a great deal of valuable information that could be employed to assess Pirenne's economic and social conclusions. Bolin, and to a lesser extent Lombard, drew attention to the Scandinavian and Russian evidence for commerce during the Carolingian era, and this was almost entirely archaeological evidence. Even Pirenne was aware of the large-scale excavations at Birka in central Sweden by the remarkable nineteenth-century archaeologist Hjalmar Stolpe (1841-1905). Stolpe found a wide range of artifacts in the burial mounds beside the trading settlement at Birka, which illuminated the role of the Vikings as intermediaries between east and west in the ninth century.[15]

Pirenne was also aware of the first systematic excavations of the trading site at Dorestad at the mouth of the Rhine. These investigations, published in 1930, demonstrated the large amount of commercial traffic along the Rhine in the

---

[15] See Anne-Sofie Graslund, *Birka IV. The burial customs*, Stockholm 1981.

Carolingian period.[16]
During the 1930s excavations began at Haithabu, near Schleswig in north Germany, another great entrepôt associated with the Carolingian economic revival. At the same time preliminary investigations were made at many rural sites of the Migration Period in Germany and Scandinavia, opening new fields of study. After the war the number of early medieval excavations increased dramatically all over Europe. The first in Southampton, for example, were undertaken in 1946-50, and new excavations were initiated in the 1950s at Hamburg, Kaupang (south-west of Oslo) and Helgö near Birka in Sweden. By this time Russian archaeologists were digging on Viking-period trading sites like Kiev and Novgorod, and by the early 1960s the first systematic excavations of medieval sites were taking place in France and Italy.[17]
During this formative period scholars evaluated the significance of these projects, and by 1960 a good deal of important work relevant to the Pirenne debate had appeared. For example, in 1937 Holger Arbman published his thesis *Schweden und das karolingische Reich*, which tried to assess the evidence of trade from Birka and other Viking sites. Similarly Herbert Jankuhn's (1936) publication of Haithabu was a landmark in early medieval studies, as were his post-war writings on North Sea and Baltic trade in the Carolingian

---

[16] J.H. Holwerda, Opgravingen van Dorestad, *Oudheidkundige Mededeelingen*, 9, 1930, 32-93.

[17] Haithabu: Herbert Jankuhn, *Haithabu. Ein handelsplatz der Wikingerzeit*, Neumünster 1976 (6th edition); Southampton: P.V. Addyman & D.H. Hill, Saxon Southampton: a review of the evidence, part1 (part 2), *Proceedings of the Hampshire Field Club*, 24-5 (26), 1968 (1969), 61-93 (61-96); Hamburg: reviewed by Uwe Lobbedey, 'Northern Germany', in M.W. Barley (ed.), *European Towns: their archaeology and history*, London 1977, 130-4; Kaupang: Charlotte Blindheim, 'Kaupang by Viks Fjord', in A.E. Herteig, H.E. Liden & C. Blindheim, *Archaeological Contributions to the Early History of Urban Communities in Norway*, Oslo 1975, 125-53; Helgö: Wilhelm Holmqvist, 'Helgö, an early trading settlement in central Sweden', in R.L.S. Bruce-Mitford (ed.), *Recent Archaeological Excavations in Europe*, London 1975, 111-32; Novgorod: M.W. Thompson, *Novgorod the Great*, London 1967; Kiev: Johann Callmer, 'The archaeology of Kiev ca. A.D. 500-1000', in R. Zeitler (ed.), *Les Pays du Nord et Byzance (Scandinavie et Byzance)*, Uppsala 1981, 29-52.

period. In the 1950s Joachim Werner, Donald Harden and Gerald Dunning each published papers on archaeological objects ascribed to the period 500-1000 and distributed round north-west Europe. Werner explored the character of the sixth- and seventh-century trading systems, while Harden published glass vessels from Early Saxon England and Dunning outlined the trade-routes implied by the distribution of Carolingian and later pots imported to Middle and Late Saxon England.[18]

Indeed by 1960 a real contrast had developed between the archaeology of the first millennium A.D. north and south of the Alps. The traditional purpose of classical archaeology in the Mediterranean was to illustrate the rise and flowering of Graeco-Roman civilisation – to provide evidence for architectural and art history – and consequently the decline and fall of Rome received scant treatment. All too often the upper archaeological levels, formed as the cities and rural dwellings of the Roman Empire fell into decay, were simply shovelled away in the pursuit of the monumental architecture and associated objects of the classical period. The trend reached a peak in Italy and north Africa under Fascism. Gigantic excavations, such as those in Rome, Ostia and Lepcis Magna, were designed to reveal the monumental achievements of the past, which Mussolini sought to emulate. Only since the war have classical archaeologists paid wholehearted attention to the latest layers in cities like Corinth, Athens, Sardis and Carthage (Fig. 2). Even today few archaeologists have explored the rural dimension of the collapse of the Roman Empire, and fewer still have gone in search of the origins of the medieval pattern of settlement.

Surprising as it may seem, the systematic excavation of Islamic sites is even more recent. Until the 1960s excavations were designed almost exclusively to uncover monumental

[18] Holger Arbman, *Schweden und das karolingische Reich*, Stockholm 1937; Joachim Werner, 'Fernhandel und Naturalwirtschaft in östlichen Merowingerreich nach archäologischen numismatischen Zengnissen', *Bericht der Romanisch-Germanisch Kommission* 42, 1961, 307-46; D.B. Harden, 'Glass vessels in Britain and Ireland, A.D. 400-1000', in D.B. Harden (ed.), *Dark Age Britain*, London 1956, 132-67; G.C. Dunning, in 'Anglo-Saxon pottery: a symposium', *Medieval Archaeology* 3, 1959, 31-78.

Fig. 2 Excavations of an Early Byzantine building at the Avenue Habib Bourgiba, Carthage, in 1976. The remains of the city wall to the right, as well as the outlines of a town house in the centre, can be seen. (Photo: Henry Hurst.)

architecture, and even today stratigraphy, statistical study of artifacts and the collection of biological data, such as bones or seeds, are the exception rather than the rule.

Nevertheless the past twenty years have been a revolutionary period for archaeology in general. Since 1960 there has been, to paraphrase one historian, a floodtide of excavations and related archaeological studies. Archaeology has expanded so much that another historian wondered whether it might not be a scholarly manifestation of the new materialistic age.[19] In fact there are complex reasons for the growth and maturing of the subject. In Europe and the United States, urban and rural redevelopment continues to threaten our archaeological heritage on an unprecedented scale. Survey and salvage excavation have been required as never before, and consequently many of the larger towns in England, Wales, Scotland, Ireland, the Netherlands, West Germany,

[19] See, for example, Moses Finley, *Ancient Sicily*, London 1979 (2nd edition), xii; and R. Allen Brown, 'An historian's approach to the origins of the castle in England', *Archaeological Journal* 126, 1970, 132.

Denmark, Norway and Sweden have been subjected to at least some archaeological scrutiny. Some centres – Aarhus, Amsterdam, Cologne, London, Oslo, Tours, Winchester and York, for example – have been the scene of massive excavations, yet to be fully published. The expansion of archaeology has had various spin-offs. Expeditions have set out to work in the Mediterranean in greater numbers than ever before, while others have gone further afield to developing countries – the successors of the archaeological missions which began work in the nineteenth century. Active fieldwork has also generated research on finds, and on the physical characteristics of archaeological materials of every kind. The development of radiocarbon dating is the best-known result of the collaboration of scientists and archaeologists, but other techniques such as dendrochronology – the building up of a sequence of highly precise dates from the identifiable tree rings of preserved timbers – have been perfected (Fig. 3). All sorts of techniques have recently developed to identify the places of origin of pots, glass or metal objects, and to establish the similarity of one object to another, so that the distribution of traded goods can be plotted.

The intensification of archaeological research has proceeded hand in hand with a revolution in archaeological thinking.[20] In the 1960s a number of archaeologists were greatly influenced by theoretical and methodological developments in anthropology, biology, geography and mathematics. The so-called 'New Archaeologists' tried to introduce concepts from allied fields and then set out to discover the means of testing these hypotheses in the field. Their chief purpose was to turn archaeology into a science and in particular to search for patterns in human behaviour in the past. Only archaeology, they argued, was in a position to examine long-term human developments and to compare such developments on a global basis.

In a sense this theoretical revolution was made possible by computers, which enable us to analyse large quantities of archaeological data quickly, but the fundamental difference

[20] A concise review of these developments will be found in Bruce Trigger, *Time and Traditions: essays in archaeological interpretation*, Edinburgh 1978.

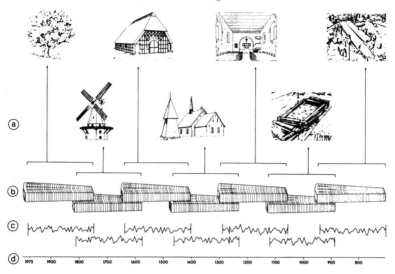

Fig. 3 The dendrochronological sequence used to date the early ninth-century timbers found at Haithabu, northern Germany. (Courtesy Prof. D. Eckstein)

between the New Archaeologists and their predecessors lies in their premise that archaeology is the past tense of anthropology. Understandably American archaeologists have been the standard-bearers of this crusade, coming as they do from departments of anthropology rather than archaeology, for in America many archaeology departments tend to focus on the study of art history. Of course, the archaeological 'old guard', together with some historians, have been wary of the shift towards generalising models of human behaviour, but they should bear in mind that the same archaeologists have been developing 'middle range theory' in order to recognise and interpret patterns of archaeological evidence appropriate to testing general theories. This is leading to far-reaching improvements in programmes of fieldwork, a greater interest in regional studies rather than single-site excavations, and a keen awareness of the question of sampling the archaeological record. There is an increase, too, in the number of environmentalists in archaeological projects – a recognition that man's relations with man are only one dimension of life on earth. The debates continue, and there is no sign that this theoretical revolution is coming to an end. Indeed it has made converts in most parts of the globe, who are conspicuous in initiating changes in the scope of archaeological study in every continent. Today most of them would challenge 'old-fashioned' historians, who in a sense have dominated archaeological theory for a century, and contend that the humanists have inhibited the development of the subject.

How can the New Archaeology shed light on the relations between two historical figures, such as Mohammed and Charlemagne? Indeed can archaeologists offer useful comments on changing economies and their social implications, when there are precise chronological constraints which are fundamental to the debate? The answer to the first question will be found in the chapters which follow, and at the end the reader must judge for himself. The answer to the second must be given now, for it is fundamental to the argument we present.

Archaeologists, we maintain, *are* in a position to make useful judgments on historical issues relating to social and economic change, provided that our means of dating the evidence is sufficiently precise. In the medieval period the evidence is often well dated, especially now that certain key sites have been reconsidered in the light of dendrochronological studies of the timbers found in modern excavations. We have benefited too from the frequent reassessments of medieval coinage by analytical methods, which ascertain the metal content of particular coins or hoards. Most of all we have benefited from the persistent refinement of ceramic sequences in Europe and Asia, enabling us to associate minor sites (where pottery is one of the few classes of artifacts recovered) with major sites, about which we are relatively well informed. Often, of course, the dates assigned to pottery have a wide margin of error – they are seldom closer than ± 25 years – and yet they provide us with a means of dating for all kinds of sites.

At the same time improved techniques of excavation have brought to light the ephemeral structures associated with decaying towns or poorer rural settlements. Thus we can now talk about the decline of Rome in archaeological terms and begin to comment on settlements in all parts of Europe, Asia Minor and north Africa in this critical period. Moreover the

Fig. 4 Field survey in the upper Volturno valley, central Italy. (Photo: Richard Hodges)

finds from these ephemeral features enable us to recognise contemporary sites, even when they survive only as scatters of pottery, tile and other refuse (Fig. 4). And so it is now theoretically – and often actually – possible to recognise the devolution of settlement patterns as the world of Late Antiquity took on the characteristics of the Middle Ages. In other words we are at last beginning to appreciate exactly when the topography of the medieval world – unchanged till recently – was formed. How and why this topography came about – the new arrangements of dwellings, communities, villages and towns – is an altogether separate issue, which should be discussed with historians, who draw upon contemporary documents. None the less all settlement patterns reflect the socio-economic systems which created them and which they then helped to modify. Thus excavations in a twentieth-century region that revealed bits of a petrol station, minor sections of a factory complex, rubbish heaps, dwellings and so forth, in conjunction with a spatial representation of settlements and their individual size, would tell us what kind of socio-economic system prevailed. Similarly archaeological research shows how the agrarian market-oriented economy of the Roman period conforms to a well-known geographic pattern, in which one expects to find the ranked tiers of markets within each region, with every settlement, in theory, being a function of an all-embracing system. By contrast, in a society in which markets do not exist, or exist only as a minor feature, the patterns of settlement will have an altogether different form. In this situation, the settlement pattern will be determined by the political system, and quite possibly by ecological factors. Archaeologists have been developing their research on pre-market settlement patterns because their evidence of these is much better than the evidence available to geographers or anthropologists working in the last century. The documentary historian seldom if ever has such spatial details before the Renaissance, when maps were compiled in quantity, and so in this respect the archaeological evidence of medieval settlement patterns is of paramount importance.[21] In much the same way (using the crudest calculations) we have been paying far greater attention to the production of goods in order to discover whether technology and output can throw light on the nature of one type of economy or another. We have also become attentive to patterns of artifact distribution which may be associated with the different types of economic systems. The type of manufacture and the pattern of traded goods within a society in which the market-place system prevails should be entirely different from those patterns arising in pre-market contexts where basic needs and certain social requirements have to be met. The mass-production of pottery by inter-regional and regionally based kilns is a feature of market societies, while at the other end of the economic spectrum simple hand-made pottery restricted to individual settlements illustrates an entirely different regime.

The important feature to remember when we discuss such typologies of economic systems reflected in archaeological remains is that there are more than three or four such patterns known from world prehistory and history, and that our appreciation of such things is constantly becoming finer: it is scarcely relevant to describe the vestiges of the Roman Empire in terms derived from anthropological fieldwork in Polynesia. The New Archaeology has forced the pace in refining theoretical   concepts,   and   many   recent   papers   in

[21] Richard Hodges, *Dark Age Economics: the origins of towns and trade A.D. 600-1000*, London 1982, 15-20.

Mesoamerican or Mesopotamian archaeology are especially helpful when we are reconsidering the range of earlier excavated material with our modern, scientifically acquired data relating to the European Dark Ages.

Of course it would be worthless to use *only* the new archaeological evidence to investigate the Pirenne thesis. The archaeological data must be considered together with the historical and numismatic evidence. Nevertheless we believe that the archaeological data provide a valuable new means of approaching the debate about the origins of Europe, especially when this evidence is considered in what might be called anthropological terms. We are well aware that there is wide scope for improving all aspects of the archaeological information described in the following pages; but we believe that enough new data have come to light to revive the debate. Pirenne himself would surely have approved, not least because there seems to have been more to his famous dictum than even he perceived. Without Mohammed, Charlemagne would indeed have been inconceivable.[22]

[22] Henri Pirenne, op. cit., 234.

2. The Decline of the Western Empire

Pirenne drew two sweeping conclusions:

1. The Germanic invasions destroyed neither the Mediterranean unity of the ancient world, nor what may be regarded as the truly essential features of the Roman culture as it still existed in the fifth century ...
2. The cause of the break with the tradition of antiquity was the rapid and unexpected advance of Islam ...[1]

The purpose of this chapter and the next is to examine these conclusions, which summarise the first part of his book.

The historical setting

In 376 a confederacy of Alans, Goths and Huns crossed the Imperial frontier and advanced into Thrace. In 378 the Eastern Emperor Valens confronted them at Adrianople, barely 200 kilometres from his capital, Constantinople. The Emperor was killed, but the invaders could not agree what to do next and dispersed. The capital was spared, but the disaster served as a bitter foretaste of what was to come.[2]

The death of the Western Emperor Theodosius I in 395 probably provided the incentive for a new offensive. This time the confederacy was led by the king of the Visigoths, Alaric, who penetrated as far as the Peloponnese in 397 and through some timely political bargaining was made commander of Imperial troops in the north-west Balkans. This was disastrous for the Western Empire, for in 401 or 2 Alaric invaded Italy. After an indecisive battle with the Emperor of the West, Honorius, he retreated, but returned in 408/9, when he and his

[1] Henri Pirenne, *Mohammed and Charlemagne*, London 1939, 284.
[2] A.H.M. Jones, *The Later Roman Empire*, Oxford 1964.

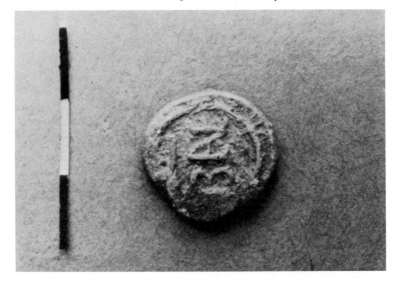

Fig. 5 A seventh-century lead coin from Luni, north Italy (scale in cms) (Photo: Bryan Ward-Perkins)

army laid siege to Rome and, despite repeated negotiations, sacked it in 410. The Western government had withdrawn to the security of Ravenna, but its prestige was tarnished permanently by the Visigoths' success. In fact, Alaric's men did comparatively little damage before leaving Rome and marching south. They intended to cross to Africa, but Alaric died before they could sail, and under his brother-in-law's leadership the Visigoths were persuaded to turn and head for Gaul, this time as champions of the Western Empire. In Gaul the Visigoths counterbalanced a confederacy of Alans, Suebi and Vandals, and a fragile peace ensued. But within a few years they aimed once again for Africa, failed, chose Spain instead and finally, at the Emperor's invitation, settled in Aquitaine in 418. Here they assumed the role of 'official' settlers, contributing in some measure to the preservation of local stability.

In the 420s the Vandals under Gaiseric crossed the Straits of Gibraltar and proceeded along the African coast. They arrived at Carthage in 435 and made this great port their capital. Hostile contemporaries criticised the Vandals for persecuting the Christians of North Africa and making coastal raids which extended to the shores of southern Italy and Sicily. Modern historians have claimed that Carthage fell into decay as merchants sought safer harbours; we discuss the problem below on pp. 26-30.

In Gaul, the Visigoths eventually expanded their Aquitainian kingdom into Provence, while the Alans settled in the upper Rhone valley and the Burgundians in Savoy. In 447, however, Attila led the Huns across the Danube and attempted to hold the West to ransom. Four years later an alliance of Romans and newly settled barbarians met the Huns in battle near Troyes and forced Attila to retreat. The Huns then swept briefly into Italy, but Attila died in 453 and the Hunnish threat evaporated. In the next 40 years the Franks secured most of northern France (see Chapter 4), and the Alemanni extended their territory to embrace Alsace and the northern Alps. Gaiseric's Vandals fell on Rome and, in the confusion that followed, the Visigoths migrated to Spain and carved out a kingdom which extended from the Massif Central to Gibraltar. At the end of the period the Skirian general Odoacer became King of Italy and established a period of local stability from 476 to 488.

This period of calm was shattered when Theodoric marched his Ostrogothic followers into Italy at the instigation of the Eastern Emperor, Zeno. Theodoric overwhelmed Odoacer's forces and executed him in 493. Italy then enjoyed three comparatively peaceful decades until Theodoric's death in 526. Theodoric stemmed the expansion of the Franks into Provence under Clovis, but contented himself with Italy as a kingdom. He died without an adult male heir, and under his daughter, the regent Amalosuntha, the kingdom began to crumble. Less than a decade later the new Eastern Emperor Justinian was engaged in a crusade to rid the West of the barbarians. In 534 his general, Belisarius, captured Carthage, and the Vandals vanished as a political entity. In 536 Belisarius invaded Italy, and by 540 the Ostrogothic capital, Ravenna, was in his hands. But Justinian's triumph was short-lived, for a Sasanian army from Iran swept into Syria, and though his armies landed in Spain in the 550s decisive victory against the well-established Visigoths eluded them.

Justinian's conquests in the West did not last. The Spanish territory was ceded by the 620s when the Sasanian invasion made it impossible to defend his westernmost possession. The Balkans were overrun by Slavs in the 570s and 580s, and in Greece the coastal ports lost their mountainous hinterlands. The North African possessions lasted longer, as we shall see, but Italy soon fell to a new barbarian group, the Lombards.

The Lombards had been invited to Italy in 552 to aid Justinian against the Ostrogoths. In 568 their king, Alboin, decided to consolidate his power while Italy was vulnerable in the aftermath of Justinian's death – his own people faced annihilation at the hands of the Avars if they remained in central Europe. Between 568 and 571 the Lombards advanced down the peninsula, sometimes fighting the Byzantines and sometimes supporting them, creating a kingdom in the north, a dukedom around Spoleto and another around Benevento. The Byzantine counter-offensive failed to destroy the Lombard confederacy, and the peninsula became a patchwork of states, which survived in one form or another until the Risorgimento in the nineteenth century.

Long-distance trade

A cornerstone of Pirenne's first conclusion – that the Mediterranean world was essentially the same in 600 as it had been in 400 – was the continuation of trade. In the fourth century, as in earlier periods, trade was intense and commodities were moved in bulk across the length and breadth of the Mediterranean. Was this still happening in 600? As a historian, Pirenne based his case almost exclusively on written evidence, using two categories of information: on traders, and on the articles they traded.

First, the traders. Salvian (d. *c*.484) wrote of the Syrian merchants of Marseille, and Caesarius, bishop of Arles (d.542), composed hymns not only in Latin (for the local population) but in Greek (for the foreign community, presumably merchants). We hear of merchants in Spain in about 570 and of Jews, Greeks and Syrians at Narbonne in 589. As far as the merchandise is concerned, we have numerous references to goods from the eastern Mediterranean in the western provinces in the sixth century and after. Gregory of Tours (*c.*539-594), for example, mentions a bequest of wine from Gaza to a church in Lyon for use in the eucharist.[3] These snippets of information, which confirm the continuation of trade, are useful – but only up to a point. They tell us nothing about the *volume* of trade; indeed, the very fact that they mention traders and trade goods implies that we are dealing with the exception rather than the rule.

Fortunately archaeological evidence is beginning to compensate for this deficiency. Imported objects found in excavations can be quantified and used to estimate the volume of trade, while their distribution can suggest the extent of commercial networks. Let us consider three recent excavations – in Rome, Carthage and the small north Italian port of Luni – which tell us much about the economy of the fifth and sixth centuries.

Rome

The so-called Schola Praeconum (the name is modern) stands at the foot of the Palatine, overlooking the Circus Maximus. In 1978-80 excavation revealed that part of the building had been deliberately filled with earth and rubble. The fill consists of rubble from the demolition of a well-appointed building and of domestic (and possibly warehouse) rubbish. Thirty-eight legible coins show that the filling dates from the second quarter of the fifth century, perhaps from *c.* 430-40 (Fig. 6).[4]

The filling in the Schola Praeconum contained a large amount of broken pottery: 22,315 fragments, weighing 423 kilograms. A significant proportion of the pottery (44.6 per cent of the sherds, or 60 per cent of the total weight) consists of amphorae, used for the transportation and storage of perishable commodities, such as olive oil, wine and *garum* (a

[3] Gregory of Tours, *A History of the Franks* (ed. Lewis Thorpe), Harmondsworth 1974, 411.

[4] D. Whitehouse, G. Barker, R. Reece & D. Reese, 'The Schola Praeconum 1. The coins, pottery and fauna', *Papers of the British School at Rome* 50, 1982.

kind of fish sauce, which the Romans consumed in great quantities). We know enough about the characteristics of Roman amphorae and the clays from which they were made to suggest where many of the fragments originated. Here are two analyses of the pottery from the Schola Praeconum, with particular reference to the amphorae:

Class of pottery	% fragments	% weight
Domestic	10.6	8.5
Amphorae	44.6	60.0
Not classified	44.8	31.5
Total	100.0	100.0

Type of amphora	% fragments	% weight
North African	42.5	63.0
Biv	20.5	6.9
Bii	19.2	14.7
Others	17.8	15.4
Total	100.0	100.0

The three most common types of amphora – North African, Biv and Bii – come from three different parts of the Mediterranean. The North African amphorae, which have a distinctive brick-red fabric, sometimes with a white surface, were imported from Tunisia. It has always been assumed that they contained olive oil, and recent analyses of lipid residues embedded in the fabric of sherds from the Schola Praeconum have shown this assumption to be correct.[5] Biv amphorae also have a distinctive fabric: they are deep brown in colour, with abundant mica and a 'soapy' texture. The characteristics of the clay suggest that they were made in western Turkey,

[5] S. Passi, M.C. Rothschild-Boros, P. Fasella, M. Nazzaro-Porro & D. Whitehouse, 'An application of high performance liquid chromatography to analysis of lipids in archaeological samples', *Journal of Lipid Research* 22, 1981, 778-84.

Fig. 6 A general view of the Schola Praeconum, Rome. (Photo: David Whitehouse)

perhaps in the Meander valley. Bii amphorae also come from the east, possibly from Antioch in Syria. The amphorae from the Schola Praeconum, therefore, indicate the continuing existence of large-scale seaborne trade between Rome, North Africa and the eastern Mediterranean, in about 430-40. They also provide our first illustration of the importance of pottery when discussing commerce.

Carthage

The Schola Praeconum provides an insight into the long-distance trade of Rome in the fifth century; Carthage widens the discussion. The leading Punic and Roman port of the Maghreb, Carthage, was the capital of the imperial province of Africa until it fell to the Vandals in 438. Before this most of the vast crop of North African corn destined for Italy passed through Carthage, as did huge quantities of olive oil. Historians have argued that Gaiseric's seizure of Carthage curtailed Rome's access to her traditional granary and that alternative supplies were needed until Belisarius recaptured the city for Justinian in 534. Massive excavations sponsored

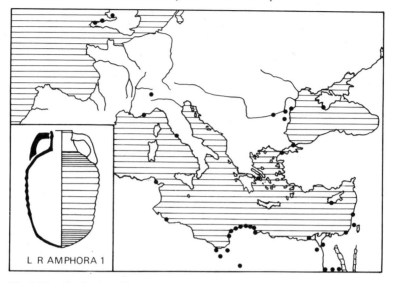

L R AMPHORA 1

Fig. 7 The distribution of later Roman amphora type 1 (as defined at Carthage by John Riley). Note the incidence of these vessels in south-west Britain. (After John Riley)

by UNESCO have made it possible to examine the traditional picture (Fig. 2). The American and British teams, in particular, have concentrated on the latest phases of occupation. In the process both teams have been forced to handle vast amounts of pottery, including hundreds of thousands of amphora sherds and African Red Slip (ARS) tablewares (Fig. 7). The preliminary analyses of these many different types of pottery, in conjunction with parallel studies of the coins, have induced M.J. Fulford and John Riley to offer alternative interpretations for Carthage's final centuries.[6]

Fulford writes as follows:

In the early fifth century (*c*.400-425), only about 10 per cent of the amphorae can be assigned to East Mediterranean

[6] M.J. Fulford, 'Carthage: overseas trade and the political economy, *c.* A.D. 400-700', *Reading Medieval Studies* 6, 1980, 68-80; J.A. Riley, 'The pottery from the cisterns 1977. 1, 1977.2 and 1977.3', in J.H. Humphrey (ed.), *Excavations at Carthage 1977 Conducted by the University of Michigan*, Ann Arbor 1981, 85-124.

sources. This percentage is doubled by c.A.D. 475-500 and, in the groups deposited at about the time of Belisarius' invasion ..., 25-30 per cent of all the amphorae can certainly be attributed to sources in the East Mediterranean.

Riley arrived at the same conclusion. But surprisingly both have shown that after 534 the proportion of imported to local amphorae in Carthage dropped dramatically, and that by about 600 the incidence of eastern Mediterranean amphorae is in fact negligible. The impression that Carthage enjoyed a buoyant economy in the late fifth and early sixth centuries is to some extent confirmed by the large numbers of high quality tablewares (African Red Slip wares) found in the excavations. Finally, Fulford points out that Vandal coinage issued in Carthage was widely circulated around the Mediterranean. By contrast, after Justinian re-established an imperial mint at Carthage, coins from other mints in the eastern Mediterranean found in the city amount to a tiny fraction of the numismatic collection as a whole. 'Out of more than 325 Byzantine coins catalogued from the American excavations,' writes Fulford, 'only eight are from eastern mints, two from Sicily and two from Constantine in Numidia', and he shows that the Carthaginian issues minted after 533 are rare around the Mediterranean.[7]

Fulford interprets this new archaeological evidence in an imaginative way. He argues that once the province was released from its obligation to Rome, it was possible to sustain a lively trading relationship with various parts of the Mediterranean. Although in practice agricultural production within the province may have fallen, great emphasis was still placed on commerce, because the surplus was no longer exported as tax or invested in monumental buildings. There is certainly some evidence of a decline of estates in the fifth century. However, once Justinian reconquered the city and it was again burdened with taxes, commercial life diminished and the corn sold for private luxuries under the Vandals was requisitioned to meet the needs of the state.

[7] Fulford, op. cit., 71; 74.

Fig. 8 Seventh-century burials cut into an earlier building close to the city wall of Carthage. (Photo: Henry Hurst)

The last phases of occupation in several buildings near the city wall betray the pitiful condition of Carthage in the seventh century.[8] The British excavators uncovered a comparatively well-preserved mud-brick building, L-shaped in form, dating from the late sixth or early seventh century. After its abandonment the zone was used as a burial ground. Henry Hurst, the excavator, writes that 'late burials occur commonly within the former urban area of Carthage, as in other sites of Byzantine Africa, and are conventionally interpreted as representing a late stage of decline, economically and in terms of population, when large areas of the city were redundant and the traditional regulations requiring burial areas to be outside the city walls were relaxed' (Fig. 8). A further building over this graveyard has been interpreted as the home of refugees from the Arabs, who arrived in the province in 695-8. By then, the city was only a shadow of its former self and must have resembled the decaying industrial towns with which, today, we in the West are beginning to become familiar.

Luni

The later history of Luni, a small Roman town near La Spezia, is strikingly similar to that of Carthage. Careful excavations by Bryan Ward-Perkins in the forum at the centre of the walled town have revealed its post-classical history.[9] Until about 400 Luni's wealth was principally derived from the export of Luna (Carrara) marble, quarried nearby. The decline of the marble trade must have had a devastating effect on the town, but nevertheless it survived in Byzantine hands until 640, when eventually it fell to the Lombards. Under

---

[8] Henry Hurst, 'Excavations at Carthage 1977-8. Fourth interim report', *Antiquaries Journal* 59, 1979, 19-49, esp. 44-6.

[9] Bryan Ward-Perkins, 'Luni – the decline of a Roman town', in H. McK. Blake, T.W. Potter & D.B. Whitehouse (eds), *Papers in Italian Archaeology* 1, Oxford (B.A.R. supplementary series 41) 1978, 313-21; 'Luni: the prosperity of the town and its territory', in G. Barker and R. Hodges (eds), *Archaeology and Italian Society*, Oxford (B.A.R. International Series 102) 1981, 179-90; 'Two Byzantine houses at Luni', *Papers of the British School at Rome* 49, 1981, 91-8.

Lombard rule it remained a diocesan centre until 1201-4 when the bishopric was moved to Sarzana. The recent excavations have uncovered the vestigial remains of wooden structures, probably dwellings, spanning the period between the fifth and the ninth century or later, associated with deep rubbish pits and wells.

The archaeology of the latest Roman phases at Luni is particularly interesting because the excavations have been so meticulous and suggest what might be found at other classical sites in the Mediterranean. The interim reports show that the post-built dwellings bear a striking resemblance to the homes of the barbarians best known, at this period, in West Germany (Fig. 9). Yet the material trampled into the thin floor surfaces and dropped in activity areas indicates that 'Byzantine' copper coinage continued in use until about 600. In addition, eastern Mediterranean amphorae and Syrian glass were being imported. After about 600, on the other hand, the material standard of life appears to have suffered a further decline – imports from other parts of the Mediterranean are rare,

Fig. 9 Remains of a sixth-century timber building at Luni, north Italy. Post-bases, post-holes and the remains of a clay floor can be seen. (Photo: Bryan Ward-Perkins)

although analysis of the refuse implies that there was no significant alteration in the diet.

Bryan Ward-Perkins contends that the town's impoverishment after the collapse of the marble trade was due in large measure to the decay of the classical drainage systems in the food-growing *territorium*. Gradually much of this territory reverted to marsh. It is clear that Luni was barely operating as a port when the Lombards ousted the last Byzantine governor in 640. The town was never abandoned, though there was no more than a cluster of Byzantine households within its walls, and these were remote from their classical predecessors in almost every respect. The excavations have aroused considerable interest, mainly because archaeologists are beginning to wonder whether the decay of Luni can be used as a model for the decay of classical towns generally in Italy. Bryan Ward-Perkins opposes this view and points to the documentary evidence for the survival of centres like nearby Lucca. Nevertheless the evidence from Luni itself is incontrovertible. Whatever happened elsewhere, the port collapsed.

These glimpses of late Roman trade suggest two working hypotheses. First, the arrival of the 'barbarians' in the late fourth and fifth centuries damaged, but did not destroy, the commerce of the central and western Mediterranean: Rome continued to import oil and wine (and many other things) after the Gothic invasion; under the Vandals, Carthage may actually have experienced a boom in trade with the East; Luni was still receiving foreign goods in the sixth century. As we shall see in Chapter 4, the spin-off from Mediterranean trade in the time of Theodoric arrived (in the form of coins and metal vessels) as far north as Sweden. Secondly, however, the situation had changed completely by about 600: Carthage had virtually ceased trading with the East and at Luni imported luxuries disappeared.

Admittedly these are large hypotheses built on flimsy evidence. The excavation of a tiny fraction of Carthage and an even smaller fraction of Rome, one might object, is hardly significant. And what of Luni, a minor town dependent on a single product – marble? Well, the decline of the marble trade itself speaks volumes and, as we shall see in Chapter 3, the pattern we suggest in the central Mediterranean is not dissimilar from the pattern emerging in the East. In any case, the hypothesis that intensive long-distance trade and the market economy collapsed in the sixth century can be tested by a study of rural settlement in Dark Age Italy.

Rural settlement in Italy

The acid test of major social and economic change is its detection on a regional scale. Individual centres such as Rome, Carthage or Luni might survive or decline for highly individual reasons, but the fortunes of villas and peasant holdings should reflect economic trends of a more general kind. We must ask therefore: When was the classical pattern of settlement and land-use succeeded by the medieval pattern?

The dating of rural settlement, especially small-holdings, is notoriously difficult because of the rarity of the closely datable objects that occur much more commonly in urban contexts. Coins, in particular, are scarce on rural sites, since they were used less frequently than in towns. This being so, the principal

Fig. 10 An African Red Slip ware dish (Hayes type 104a), dating to *c*.530-80, from Farfa in central Italy. (Photo: David Whitehouse)

Fig. 11 A Forum ware pitcher from the Lacus Iuturnae, Rome. (Photo: David Whitehouse)

means of dating late Roman farms and villas is the pottery. In practice this means that we use the well-studied fine wares, which are found in urban contexts with coins and are therefore datable. In the Mediterranean we have come to use North African Red Slip ware (ARS) to date the remains of the last two centuries of classical settlement (Fig. 10). In 1972 J.W. Hayes published an invaluable analysis of all the varieties of ARS together with the evidence for their distribution and date.[10]

[10] J.W. Hayes, *Late Roman Pottery*, London 1972; *Supplement to Late Roman Pottery*, London 1980.

Fig. 12 A Broadline red painted jug found at Altavilla Silentia with a seventh-century coin issued by the Emperor Heraclius. (Photo: Paolo Peduto)

Hayes' catalogue makes it possible to date sherds of ARS to relatively short periods, sometimes of less than a century. Indeed ARS often provides a better means of dating archaeological deposits than the minute bronze coins that were minted in Italy, Greece and Byzantium after about 400. Two other types of pottery also throw light on the chronology of rural sites. The first is a glazed ware, known as Forum ware, which is now thought to have been produced in Rome in about 600; the most frequent forms are spouted pitchers, which often have applied scales on the body and handle (Fig. 11). The second is a south Italian product, made in one form or another from the fifth century to about 1000 or later. This is the so-called 'Broadline' red painted pottery, which occurs on the sites of late Roman villas, in early Christian cemeteries and at early medieval settlements (Fig. 12). These three classes of pottery – ARS, Forum ware and Broadline painted ware – are essential to understanding the changing pattern of rural settlement.[11]

[11] D.B. Whitehouse, 'Forum ware', *Medieval Archaeology* 9, 1965, 55-63; 'Medieval painted pottery in South and Central Italy', *Medieval Archaeology* 10, 1966, 30-44; 'The medieval pottery of Rome', in H. Mck. Blake, T.W.

The central and south Italian classical landscape contained a 'dispersed settlement pattern', in contrast with the pattern of nucleated hilltop settlements of the medieval period. There are, of course, variations within both the classical and medieval patterns, and any generalisation should be treated with caution. None the less the shift from a settlement pattern consisting of villas and smallholdings in open or exposed areas to one highly concentrated on naturally defensible hilltops was very widespread indeed and is a subject eminently suited to archaeological analysis. Several archaeological surveys in Italy have focussed on this particular problem. Two are relevant to our concern with the process of socio-economic change in the world of Late Antiquity.

The first was in the area immediately north of Rome known as South Etruria (Fig. 13). This ambitious project was planned and directed by John Ward-Perkins, the Director of the British School at Rome from 1946 to 1974. The idea of the survey of South Etruria was deceptively simple. In the 1950s suburban expansion, and in particular mechanised agriculture, began to change the face of the Roman Campagna, revealing – and destroying – archaeological sites at an unprecedented rate. Ward-Perkins' response was a massive campaign of field working, designed to record the sites before they were lost forever. At the end of the campaign, well over two thousand sites had been recorded, ranging in size from isolated farms to entire settlements, and in date from the Bronze Age to the Renaissance. The key to interpreting a survey consists of the datable objects – usually pottery – picked up on the surface. If there is first-century pottery, the site was occupied in the first century, and so on. The earliest parts of the South Etruria survey were completed before the publication of Hayes' catalogue of African Red Slip wares, and so the initial survey reports have to be used with caution. Five areas of South Etruria were investigated, however, using Hayes' chronology: these are Eretum, the Ager Veientanus, the Via Gabina, the

---

Potter & D.B. Whitehouse (eds), *Papers in Italian Archaeology* 1, Oxford (B.A.R. Supplementary series 41) 1978, 475-93; 'Forum ware again', *Medieval Ceramics* 4, 1980, 13-16.

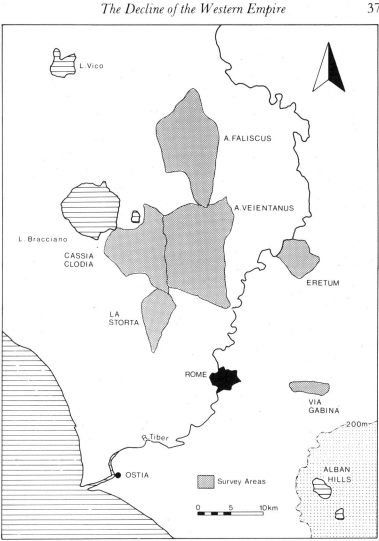

Fig. 13 South Etruria, showing the survey areas discussed on pp. 36-43.

Cassia-Clodia area and the Ager Faliscus.[12]

Hayes divided the history of ARS into three main periods on the basis of fabric. The dates of the periods are:

ARS I	*c.*80-320
ARS II	*c.*350-450
ARS III	*c.*450-625

The finds from Eretum, Ager Veientanus, Via Gabina and the Cassia-Clodia area have been published by reference to Hayes' divisions. The numbers of sites with ARS I, II and III are:

Area	ARS I	Number of sites ARS II	ARS III
Eretum	47	20	7
A. Veientanus	307	92	46
Via Gabina	27	9	6
Cassia-Clodia	57	10	6
Total	438	131	65

The standard interpretation of the data is that the Roman Campagna supported a large dispersed population until the third century, when a dramatic change began. In 1968, John Ward-Perkins summed up the situation in the Ager Veientanus as follows:

> Of the 310 [sic] sites known to have been in occupation at the end of the second century, three-quarters had vanished a century later ...; in certain marginal areas ... the proportion of sites that disappear from the record is so high that one may reasonably suggest that many of the steeper slopes were allowed to revert to pasture or woodland.[13]

[12] The most convenient overview of the many detailed papers is T.W. Potter, *The Changing Landscape of South Etruria*, London 1979. For the detailed studies see *Papers of the British School in Rome* 23, 1955; 25, 1957; 29, 1961; 30, 1962; 31, 1963; 33, 1965; 36, 1968; 40, 1972; 41, 1973; 43, 1975; 45, 1977.

[13] A. Kahane, L. Murray-Thriepland & J.B. Ward-Perkins, 'The Ager

Today there are three good reasons for asking whether the third century was indeed a period of dramatic change and, if so, whether there were others. First, such scrappy data as we possess from Rome suggest the possibility of a rapid decline in population after about 367. Secondly, the chronology of ARS has been revised since the publication of the Ager Veientanus. Thirdly – and most important of all – the dramatic contrast between the numbers of sites with ARS I and ARS II is accentuated, and the contrast between sites with ARS II and ARS III is diminished by the fact that ARS I was in use for about 240 years, ARS III for about 175 years and ARS II for only 100 years.

The survey of the Ager Faliscus, if typical, answers our first objection.[14] T.W. Potter classified the ARS by forms rather than fabrics and therefore obtained a tighter chronology, with the following result:

Date	2nd c.	3rd c.	4th c.	5-6th c.
Number of sites	95	67	31	22

The figures indicate a reduction of 29 per cent in the number of sites with ARS between the second and third centuries and a reduction of 54 per cent between the third and fourth centuries. Although this is a less dramatic picture than the reduction of 75 per cent in 100 years proposed for the Ager Veientanus, it is striking none the less; some time between the third and fourth centuries the rate of reduction in the number of sites on which ARS has been found almost doubled, from 29 per cent per 100 years to 54 per cent per 100 years.

Was this the only period of rapid decline? Let us return to the Eretum, Ager Veientanus, Via Gabina and Cassia-Clodia surveys and consider only those sites which have both *terra sigillata* and ARS I (and therefore were occupied when ARS I

Veientanus north and east of Veii', *Papers of the British School at Rome* 36, 1968, (1-218) 152.

[14] Potter, op. cit., 140.

came into use in about A.D. 80), both ARS I and ARS II (occupied *c*. 350) or both ARS II and ARS III (occupied *c*.450):

Area	Number of sites		
	c.80	*c*.350	*c*.450
Eretum	42	20	5
A. Veientanus	268	91	39
Via Gabina	22	9	6
Cassia-Clodia	45	9	3
Total	377	129	53

We are dealing now with numbers of sites known to have been occupied at given dates. Between *c*.80 and *c*.350, the numbers of known sites were reduced by between 52 per cent and 80 per cent (the average is 66 per cent) in 270 years, and the data from the Ager Faliscus suggest that the figures conceal one relatively slow and one relatively rapid period of reduction. Between *c*.350 and *c*.450, the rates of reduction were between 33 per cent and 75 per cent (the average being 41 per cent) (Fig. 14). The overall reduction between *c*.80 and *c*.450 was 86 per cent.

In round figures, therefore, the total number of small-holdings and villas known to have been occupied in the Roman Campagna seems to have fallen by well over 80 per cent between the late first century and the mid-fifth century. The decline began in the second and third centuries and for a while ran at just under 30 per cent per 100 years. It accelerated to more than 50 per cent for every hundred years between the third and fourth centuries and thereafter continued, but at a slower pace.

How can we explain the phenomenon? The possibilities are (1) quite simply, a decline in the use of ARS (our evidence, remember, consists entirely of the distribution of potsherds); (2) a change in the pattern of settlement involving the replacement of many small sites by fewer large ones; (3) migration from the countryside to the country towns; (4) migration to Rome; (5) a decline in the population of the countryside and the country towns and of Rome itself.

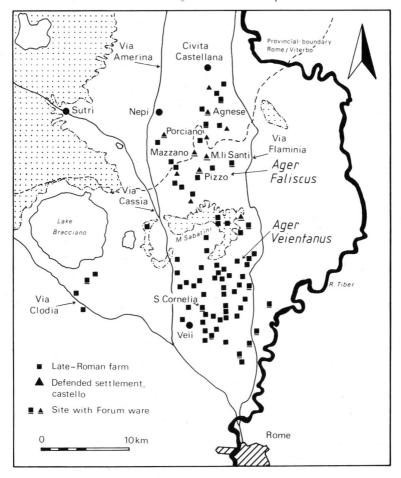

Fig. 14 Later Roman settlements found in the South Etruria survey. (After Whitehouse and Potter 1981)

None of the first three possibilities satisfactorily explains what happened. Excavations in Rome show that ARS was still common in c.430-40, and a massive decline in its importation seems improbable for most of the period in question, though the Vandal invasion of Africa may have reduced the supply and so distorted our estimate of the number of sites in c.450; indeed fifth- or sixth-century ARS has turned up on at least three excavated sites in northern Lazio. On the second possibility: while the proportion of villas to small-holdings rose, the actual number of villas declined. The change was in any case far too small to absorb all the inhabitants of the abandoned smallholdings. On the third possibility: the scarcity of ARS III and of late inscriptions at the sites of the country towns seems to imply that they, too, declined.

We are left with: (4) migration to Rome and (5) an overall reduction of population. The present evidence suggests that these were the important factors. All the information from the South Etruria survey tells the same story: an uneven, but continuous decline in the number of rural sites known to have been occupied which, if we are correct in rejecting explanations (1)-(3), represents an uneven, but continuous, decline in the rural population. Rome, on the other hand, if the figures for the dole (discussed on p. 50) are even remotely indicative, also experienced an overall decline, but with periods of growth in the fourth century and the second quarter of the fifth. These observations are consistent with the view that an overall reduction in the size of the population may have taken place between the second or third century and the mid-fifth century (and after), but that on two occasions the population of Rome was 'topped up' by immigrants from the Roman Campagna. This reduction in the total population may well have been smaller than the reduction in the number of identified sites implies, but we find it difficult to believe that *no* reduction took place.

Indeed, the decline of more than 80 per cent in the number of known sites in the Roman Campagna was not an isolated phenomenon. The Theodosian Code tells us that in Campania alone 528,042 *iugera* (1332 square kilometres) were no longer taxable and so presumably had gone out of cultivation by 395. The Visigoth invasion exacerbated the problem, and in 413 taxes on cultivated land were reduced in Campania, Tuscany, Picenum, Samnium, Bruttium, Calabria and Lucania. In 418 they were reduced again (to one ninth of the original figure) in Campania, Picenum and Tuscany. We find a similar state of affairs in Africa. In 422 the area of taxable (i.e. cultivated) land was reduced from 7425 to 3768 square kilometres in Byzacena: an overall decline of 45 per cent. Although C.R.

Whittaker reminds us that the sources are 'atrocious' and we cannot know precisely what reductions in the amount of taxable land imply for the size of the population, we find it difficult to escape the conclusion that the classical pattern of dispersed settlement was transformed in the late Imperial period.[15]

The temptation at this point is to become suspicious of the archaeological evidence for a substantial decline in population. After all, might not the disappearance of the diagnostic later sixth-century African Red Slip wares simply reflect the economic changes in the western Mediterranean? In other words, is it not possible that smaller farms that could not obtain, or simply could not afford, ARS continued to exist? Chris Wickham, reviewing the survey data from South Etruria, went so far as to state that 'generalised demographic collapse is a difficult enough process even to imagine, let alone ... locate in the evidence'. He goes on: 'What historical sources we have in the eighth century, primarily the *Liber Ponteficalis*, give no impression that the countryside had been abandoned.'[16]

What kinds of settlement were in existence as the classical pattern dissolved and, we suggest (despite Whittaker, Wickham and others), the actual size of the population declined? And when, precisely, was there a shift towards occupying hill-tops, thereby breaking with the tradition of a thousand years?

The form of the latest Roman farms in South Etruria remains something of a mystery since the only site of the period for which we have even interim reports, at Anguillara Sabazia, is something of a freak (Fig. 15). An imposing tower-like structure, built in the second century, perhaps as the country retreat of a wealthy resident of Rome, was made defensible some time in the period 450-550. Immediately outside the

[15] C.R. Whittaker, 'Agri deserti', in Moses I. Finley (ed.), *Studies in Roman Property*, Cambridge 1976, 137-65. For Africa see Denys Pringle, *The Defence of Byzantine Africa from Justinian to the Arab Conquest*, Oxford (B.A.R. International Series 99) 1981, 109-20.

[16] C.J. Wickham, 'Historical and topographical notes on early medieval South Etruria: part II', *Papers of the British School at Rome* 47, 1979, 66-95, esp. 86.

Fig. 15 The remains at Anguillara Sabazia, Lazio. The second-century ruin is to the left, and to the right can be seen the early medieval apse of a small church. (Photo: David Whitehouse)

walls, soil and rock were removed to create, on one side at least, a shallow ditch 5 metres wide. Windows on the ground floor may have been blocked; they are blocked today, but we cannot determine when this was done. Evidently bandits or a specific military threat – the Gothic invasion, perhaps – persuaded the fifth- or sixth-century inhabitants of the area to create a refuge.[17] More conventional establishments may have resembled the fifth-century complex at S. Giovanni di Ruoti in Basilicata, now being excavated by Professor Alistair Small. Rebuilt on an impressive scale in about 460, Ruoti consisted of a well-appointed residential unit, farmyard and ancillary buildings, which remained in use until about 525.[18]

The transformation of the classical pattern of dispersed settlement has proved a lively topic of debate in the case of South Etruria. Several years ago the historian T.S. Brown

[17] David Whitehouse, 'Le Mura di S. Stefano, Anguillara Sabazia (Roma). Ultima relazione provvisoria', *Archaeologia Medievale* 9, 1982, 319-22.

[18] Alistair Small, 'San Giovanni di Ruoti: some problems in the interpretation of the structures', in K. Painter (ed.), *Roman Villas in Italy*, London (British Museum occasional paper 24) 1980, 91-109.

boldly proposed that the beginnings of change lay in the later sixth or seventh century when Alboin's Lombard invasion overran Italy.[19] He encouraged archaeologists to examine hilltops overlooking the roads which may have been used first as refuges and later became permanent settlements. Archaeological evidence for precisely this type of hilltop settlement in the late sixth or seventh century has now been found on the northern edge of the South Etruria survey area. The identification of the earliest hilltop settlements was made possible by the redating of Forum ware to the period around 600. It has been suggested recently that a zone of hilltop sites, some 40 kilometres north of Rome, dates from precisely the time of the Lombard invasion when they served as parts of a system of defence in depth: a series of 'strategic hamlets', blocking the approaches to the city, one of which (at Ponte Nepesino) has just been discovered. At the same time it is clear that many of the 'lowland' settlements behind this protective screen remained in use throughout the period in question.[20]

The South Etruria survey brings us tantalizingly close to observing the transition between the 'classical' and 'medieval' landscapes. Even so the transition from classical to medieval building types is still a closed book. Similarly, at present the shift from open dispersed sites to fortified upland settlements is only explained as a defence against Lombardic invaders; this may be a satisfactory explanation for the change on the edge of the Roman Campagna, but its wider implications have to be assessed. The recent survey and related excavations in Molise, classical Samnium, in east-central Italy, have begun to provide the answers. Extensive work has been carried out in two parts of Molise by teams from the University of Sheffield. One survey area is centred on the Biferno valley, which runs from the Apennines to the Adriatic. The other zone lies in the upper Volturno valley, in the foothills of the Apennines, where the early medieval monastery of San Vincenzo al Volturno

[19] T.S. Brown, 'Settlement and military policy in Byzantine Italy', in H. Mck. Blake, T. W. Potter & D. B. Whitehouse (eds), *Papers in Italian Archaeology* 1, Oxford (B.A.R. Supplementary series 41) 1978, 323-38.

[20] David Whitehouse & Timothy Potter, 'The Byzantine frontier in South Etruria', *Antiquity* 55, 1981, 206-10.

held its estates. Several points relating to the Late Roman and Early Medieval settlement patterns can be made in advance of the final publications.[21] First, a sharp decline in the number of villas (larger farms) occurred in both zones after about 400 (a date based on ARS). After this date, only a few nucleated sites existed in the Biferno valley, together with a few tiny farmsteads nearer the Adriatic; in the Volturno region, on the other hand, only widely-spaced nucleated sites have been identified so far. At San Vincenzo itself a large nucleated complex of the fifth to sixth century has been found beneath the eighth-century monastery. It appears, however, unless here too we are being misled by the absence of ARS, that in the sixth or possibly the seventh century all – or virtually all – the open 'classical' sites were abandoned in favour of hilltop locations. Moreover here too there are signs of a dramatic decline in the population, consistent with the evidence from South Etruria, with comparatively few inhabitants occupying the tops of the hills.

The reasons for this shift are many and may never be accurately determined. Increased taxation by the Byzantine government after Justinian's reconquest of Italy might account for a phase of rural depopulation in the sixth century. Similarly, we cannot ignore the impact of the Great Plague of 542 which ravaged Byzantium and Europe.[22] If the Black Death carried off a third of the population of Europe in the fourteenth century, who knows what effect it had in the sixth? A smaller population may have felt more vulnerable and perhaps sought security on hilltops, where their homes would be more easily defensible against marauding bands. In addition, there may have been a certain amount of movement within each region to select land more suitable for producing subsistence foodstuffs than cash crops, for the decline of cities and rural markets must have had a direct impact on peasant farming generally. The replacement of the bureaucratic Roman political system by Germanic tribal elites must have

[21] Richard Hodges, 'Excavations and survey at San Vincenzo al Volturno, Molise: 1981', *Archaeologia Medievale* 9, 1982.

[22] J-N. Biraben & J. Le Goff. 'The plague in the Early Middle Ages', in R. Forster & O. Ranum (eds.), *The Biology of Man in History*, Baltimore 1975, 48-80.

Fig. 16 The hilltop settlement at Santa Maria in Città in the Biferno valley, Molise. The old bridge across the river Biferno can be seen below the superstrada. (Photo: Graeme Barker)

led to a massive diminution of local taxes, as in the case of Carthage under the Vandals. The markets and the apparatus of government diminished, farmers were compelled to provide not only basic necessities but also manufactured goods which before had been acquired by purchase or barter, and long-distance trade collapsed.

What did the new hilltop settlements look like? Excavations in the Biferno valley provide an answer. Santa Maria in Città is a prominent hilltop overlooking the river Biferno at a point where it can be forded or bridged.[23] A survey of the hill followed by small-scale excavations in 1978 revealed two small clusters of buildings inside a circuit of fortifications enclosing the summit (Fig. 16). At the highest point was a modest church. The excavations suggest that the dwellings were built up against the defences in a typical medieval form, with storage pits behind the buildings in the zone 10 to 20 metres from the

[23] Richard Hodges, Graeme Barker & Keith Wade, 'Excavations at D85 (Santa Maria in Città): an early medieval hilltop settlement in Molise', *Papers of the British School at Rome* 48, 1980, 70-124.

defences. The excavations showed that the inhabitants had access to a very limited range of manufactured goods but were able to acquire them in large quantities, while their diet was of a high standard with a mixture of livestock, cereals and legumes. It is evident, however, that the population of this settlement was by no means tightly packed into the defended area, as in the case of villages of the tenth century and later. Instead, the evidence suggests that there were no more than about fifty inhabitants to defend the timber and stone ramparts, which in reality would have required about six hundred. Indeed the investigation at Santa Maria in Città seems to show that the site was transitional between the classical villa complexes, where several households were loosely nucleated, and the hilltop villages of the Middle Ages. Eventually Santa Maria in Città was abandoned in favour of a site that still exists on the other side of the river, Guardialfiera. The latter was defended and had ready access to a larger area of good soil, now required to meet the demands of a population far in excess of fifty. Thus, while in two areas we can trace the origins of medieval vernacular architecture and the idea of hilltop villages to the sixth or seventh century, in practice it was not until the economic revival of the tenth century that these phenomena became almost universal in central and southern Italy, as a result of the process known as *incastellamento*.

Rome

And what of Rome, once the capital of the Empire? Cassiodorus, writing as Praetorian Prefect in 523-7, looked back to the time when it was a teeming metropolis:

> The great size of the population of the city of Rome in former times is clear from the fact that it required the provision of foodstuffs from distant regions to supply its needs. While the food requirements of foreign cities were met from the adjacent provinces, Rome depended on imported yields. The great extent of the walls, the seating capacity of the places of entertainment, the remarkable size of the public baths and the number of mills ... bear witness

to the hordes of citizens.[24]

The corn supply apart, Cassiodorus was thinking of the Aurelianic wall (length: 18.1 kilometres), the Colosseum and the Circus Maximus (estimated capacities: 73,000 and 300,000 respectively) and baths like those of Caracalla (area: 11 hectares) and Diocletian (area: 14 hectares). He might have added the aqueducts, for the Anio Vetus, Marcia, Claudia and Anio Novus alone delivered some 600,000 cubic metres of water per day.[25]

Estimates of the maximum size of the population vary enormously. Geoffrey Rickman offers a figure 'near to 1,000,000', based on Augustus' claim (in *Res Gestae* 15.2) that he distributed food to 320,000 urban *plebes* – by definition, adult males – in 5 B.C. Peter Brunt calculates that adult males accounted for some 35 per cent of the free population in the time of Augustus; R.P. Duncan-Jones prefers 2/7 (28.6 per cent). Brunt's figure would give us a populace of 914,000; Duncan-Jones' figure would give us 1,220,000. To arrive at the total population, we must add slaves, who did not qualify for the dole. Thus in 5 B.C. the population of Rome cannot have been far short of one million and was perhaps greater.[26]

Although the population probably declined in the interval, Mazzarino suggests a figure for the late fourth century which is roughly the same as our estimate for 5 B.C. The figure is based on the compensation paid to pork suppliers for losses in transit. Legislation of 367 states that losses were calculated at 15 per cent and compensated in kind by the payment of 17,000 amphorae of wine, one amphora being the equivalent of 70 *librae* of meat. If 15 per cent of the pork supply was (70 x 17,000) *librae*, the total was (70 x 17,000 x 100/15) or 7,933,333 *librae*. If a single ration was 25 *librae* per year, as in 419 (see

[24] Cassiodorus, *Variae* 11. 39.

[25] D.R. Blackman, 'The volume of water delivered by the four great aqueducts of Rome', *Papers of the British School at Rome* 46, 1978, 52-72.

[26] P. Brunt, *Italian Manpower, 225 B.C.-A.D. 14*, Oxford 1971, 117; R.P. Duncan-Jones, *The Economy of the Roman Empire*, Cambridge 1974, 264n.4; G. Hermansen, 'The population of Imperial Rome: the Regionaries', *Historia* 27, 1978, 129-68; S. Mazzarino, *Aspetti sociali del IV secolo*, Rome 1951, 230-38; Rickman, *The Corn Supply of Ancient Rome*, Oxford 1980.

below), the number of recipients was 7,933,333/25, or 317,333; it was 320,000 under Augustus.

Mazzarino converts the number of recipients into the total populace by following Beloch and assuming that every 1,000 adult males imply 796 women and 137 children (i.e. that adult males were 51.7 per cent of the total). (317,333 x 100/51.7) is 613,405. After allowing for slaves and temporary residents, Mazzarino arrives at a total population of between 800,000 and 1,000,000. If we use the formulae of Brunt or Duncan-Jones, the figure rises. In 367, therefore, the dole size suggests that once again the population was almost one million.

Cassiodorus makes it clear that the population had fallen by his day, and five hundred years later it was negligible, by Augustan standards; J.C. Russell guesses 30,000 in the tenth century.[27] Regular importation of grain ceased in the seventh century, and Lazio itself probably supplied most of the city's food. Towards the end of the eighth century the *Liber Pontificalis* records that the papal estate at Capracorum, only 15 kilometres from the town, supplied staples that Imperial Rome had obtained from all over the Mediterranean: grain, wine and olive oil.

Where, then, we may ask, between the poles of a large population dependent on imported food (as in 367) and a small population supplied locally (as in the eighth century), did Rome stand in Late Antiquity?

Our main source of information on Rome itself is the Theodosian Code, which includes legislation governing the supply of free bread and meat. Two rescripts concern the period in question; one was issued in 419, the other in 452. The first established that householders were entitled to a monthly ration of pork five times a year and that 4,000 rations were to be distributed daily. The official number of recipients in 419, therefore, was (4,000 x 30) or 120,000. The second rescript established that Rome should be provided with 3,628,000 *librae* of pork a year, of which 3,528,000 *librae* were to be distributed free at the rate of 5 *librae* per month, five

[27] J.C. Russell, *Late Ancient and Medieval Population* (Transactions of the American Philosophical Society, New Series 48/3), Philadelphia 1958, 73; 93.

times a year. The official number of recipients in 452, therefore, was 3,528,000/25, or 141, 120.[28]

The following estimates emerge if we calculate the size of the populace by equating householders with adult males and using the ratios proposed (admittedly for other periods) by Brunt, Duncan-Jones and Mazzarino:

Date	Recipients	Populace according to percentage of recipients		
		28.6%	35%	51.7%
419	120,000	419,568	342,857	232,108
452	141,120	493,427	403,200	272,959

If we assume that the populace amounted to roughly 80 per cent of the population (as apparently under Augustus), we can reach the following estimates for the number of inhabitants of Rome:

Date	Population if recipients = x % populace		
	28.6%	35%	51.7%
419	524,475	428,571	290,135
452	616,783	504,000	341,198

It is not unreasonable, therefore, to guess that the population of Rome was 400,000± 25 per cent in 452. In 523-7, Cassiodorus implied that it was considerably smaller, and between the sixth and the ninth centuries the population was whittled down to a few tens of thousands. All these estimates, however, depend on fragmentary (and uncheckable) information. It would be foolish to take any of the figures as 'accurate'. Nevertheless they do give us the strong impression that Rome at its greatest extent contained more than a million people; that the population was half, or less than half, that figure in the mid-fifth century; and that after this date it declined very sharply indeed. The process, although erratic –

[28] C. Pharr, *The Theodosian Code and Novels and the Sirmondian Constitution*, Princeton 1952.

Procopius 7.22.9 claims that Rome was abandoned at one stage of the Gothic war – was inexorable.

Summary

We have investigated the decline of the classical world in the heart of the Western Empire and stand by the two hypotheses advanced above. Archaeological evidence confirms Pirenne's belief that Alaric's assault on Rome in 410 was simply one incident in a long and complex process. Excavations in Carthage, Rome, Luni and elsewhere in Italy have demonstrated the persistence of commercial life (albeit on a diminishing scale) within the Mediterranean until the sixth century. But the growing evidence from both urban and rural excavations compels us to look for the final degradation of Rome in the sixth century and to see the Arab advance after 630 as the consequence rather than the cause of the catastrophe.
    Archaeology supports the historical impression that, after a brief resurgence in the mid to late fifth century, an irreversible decline set in. The size of towns and standard of urban housing fell in a way that would have been inconceivable to the administrators of the early Empire; the economic basis of Justinian's reunified Empire was short-lived and soon seen to be hollow. The metamorphosis from the classical to the medieval system had begun. The Byzantines levied heavy taxes to pay for the army and central government in a time of almost continuous warfare, while agricultural and industrial production declined and social unrest, mass-movements and perhaps also plague led to a sizeable depopulation of the countryside. Urban life resisted a little longer, propped up, we suspect, as much by individual commercial activity as by the local bureaucracy. But this, too, was doomed by Justinian's taxes. The system gradually wound down. The instability of the countryside, now revealed by regional surveys, such as those in South Etruria and Molise, provided the opportunity for kings and tribal chiefs from north of the Alps to carve out new territories in the Mediterranean and allowed them to establish their own social and economic systems. These systems were described by late classical writers as less innovative than perhaps they were, and Pirenne too laid heavy emphasis on the survival of Roman institutions. We beg to

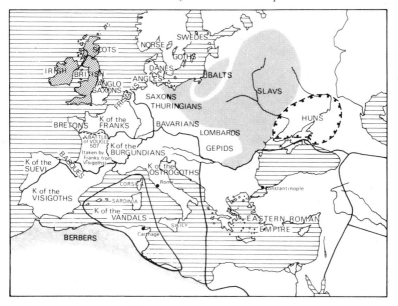

Fig. 17 The western world in the early sixth century A.D.

differ. By the end of the sixth century, conditions in the western Mediterranean bore little resemblance to those in the second century. Before the Arabs arrived, the transformation was virtually complete.

Historians – rightly – are sceptical about the idea of a 'generalised demographic decline' that lasted for centuries. After all, though the Black Death slaughtered one European in three, the population was restored to its former level within two or three generations. The Black Death, however, destroyed only people. An alternative analogy for the Mediterranean in Late Antiquity is South America in the sixteenth century, where the conquistadors not only slaughtered on a massive scale, but also destroyed the traditional social and economic systems. The result was indeed generalised demographic collapse. In the Mediterranean, the structure of Roman society and its economy were undermined, and its wealth was absorbed by two centuries of intermittent warfare. Depopulation, therefore, is not impossible; the ruined towns and wasted countryside suggest that it happened in the Mediterranean at the end of the Roman period – and the burden of proof rests with those who maintain that it didn't.

3.   The Eastern Mediterranean, 500-850

The decline of the Eastern Roman Empire began effectively with the death of Justinian (565). Justinian had re-established a unified control over the Mediterranean, but at an enormous cost. Procopius in his *Secret History* leaves us in little doubt about the financial implications of the Emperor's ambitions. The castles and forts constructed to control his vast territory meant increased taxation for a population suffering from successive waves of barbarian incursions as well as from plagues. The mosaics in his north Italian capital at Ravenna – especially those in San Vitale – reveal an Indian summer. Although Justin II (565-78) and Maurice (assassinated in 602) sustained Byzantine prowess against the ever-present threats posed by the Sasanians to the east and the Avars to the north, Italy was lost within a decade of Justinian's death, and most of Greece was overrun early in the 580s by the Slavs.

The palace revolution of 602, when Maurice and his family were put to the sword, was the first of many acts of treachery surrounding the Byzantine throne. Before Heraclius, son of the governor of Carthage, gained control in 610, the Sasanians had swept into Anatolia. In 611 Antioch fell, in 613 Damascus; next year Jerusalem was sacked and its Patriarch taken prisoner. In the following years the coastal cities of the Aegean were attacked and looted. In 619 Egypt was lost briefly, and with it Alexandria, by this time the centre of African and Asiatic commerce and the principal source of Byzantium's grain. In 626 Constantinople itself was besieged by a confederacy of Sasanians and Avars. The great walls of the city, built by Theodosius II in the earlier part of the fifth century, withstood the siege, and the Emperor Heraclius began a counter-attack, defeating the Sasanians in a battle near Mosul. Heraclius' victory distracted the world from the birth of a religious and political movement which was to overwhelm large parts of Asia and North Africa: Islam. When the prophet Mohammed died in 632, he was barely known beyond the Hejaz. Nevertheless his movement, reinforced by the economic conditions in the Arabic peninsula, produced an explosion almost without parallel. Within a century Islam had tens of millions of subjects from the Atlantic to the Indus.

Attacking simultaneously on several fronts, small bodies of mounted zealots ripped into the old Empires of Byzantium and Persia. By 640 the Byzantines had lost Palestine and Syria; in 642 they lost Alexandria; between 673 and 677 Constantinople faced a series of attacks; in 698 it was the turn of Carthage. Twelve years later the Arabs crossed to Spain and struck northwards, into Provence. About the same time, in 717, Constantinople faced its most serious siege yet, which lasted twelve months through a severe winter, after which the Arabs withdrew. Leo III (717-41), the newly crowned Emperor, held the city: we may speculate whether

Fig. 18 A medallion struck by the Emperor Justinian on conquering the Romans, 534-38. Electrotype of gold original, formerly in the Cabinet des Médailles, Paris. (Photo: David Whitehouse)

this or the victory of Charles Martel at Poitiers in 732 was the event that symbolised the end of the Arab expansion in the west. In the mid eighth century the vast Islamic 'empire' suffered its first political strains and the Umayyad dynasty of caliphs was overthrown by the Abbasids, who shifted the Islamic capital to Baghdad. The Abbasids, as we shall see in Chapter 6, chose to look in almost every direction but west – and their neglect contributed to the century of stagnation which the Mediterranean was to experience.

By 700, the Byzantine empire was reduced to Constantinople, Asia Minor and a few coastal fringes in Greece and Italy. Its great cornlands were irretrievably lost, its commercial network destroyed. Political factions and deep-rooted religious quarrels prevented any imperial aspiration to revive the Eastern Empire, and reconquest of the West was inconceivable. The coronation of Charlemagne in Rome on Christmas Day 800 was viewed with rancour, but could not be prevented. Preoccupied with the religious issue of Iconoclasm, the Byzantine court chose virtually to ignore Charlemagne and pursued a course of violent internal disagreement.

In general, historians have ignored the real state of the Byzantine economy during the Dark Ages. Most have tended to take the incidental references to towns or trade at face value.[1] In other words, until recently there existed a largely untested belief that Byzantium's economy continued for centuries along old lines – indeed that it was something of a model for the kings of barbarian Europe to emulate. But the more one looks into the archaeological evidence, the more distorted the belief appears. Although the archaeology of Dark Age Byzantium is still in its infancy, it has much to tell us when it is seen in terms of developments in the West.

The archaeological evidence

The end of Olympia in the Peloponnese is a startling case of

---

[1] See Norman Baynes' critical comments reviewed on this subject in his review of F. Lot, *La Fin du Monde Antique et le debut du Moyen Age*, Henri Pirenne, *Les Villes du Moyen Age*, et M. Rostovtzeff, *The Social and Economic History of the Roman Empire* in *Journal of Roman Studies* 19, 1929, 224-35.

classical decline. In late antiquity, the ancient city was covered by a deep deposit of alluvium composed of fine sand and silt, with lenses and beds of rounded gravel. Many monumental structures were completely buried by this wash of riverine material. E.N. Gardiner and Elsworth Huntingdon suggested that Olympia's dramatic end came when the river Kladeos was blocked by landslips provoked by earthquakes in 522 and 557. One of the buried buildings, however, is a small Justinianic fortress in which coins of 565 and 575 were found, indicating that the city's demise happened a little later. So what was responsible for the alluvium, and what does it signify? The answer was proposed by Claudio Vita-Finzi in an important essay on Mediterranean valleys.[2] He showed that an almost universal feature of the river valleys of the Mediterranean basin in the period 400-900 was the formation of an alluvial deposit which he calls the Younger Fill. He identified this deposit not only at Olympia, where it was brought down by the river Kladeos, but in many other Greek, Italian, Palestinian, North African and Spanish valleys (Fig. 19). The origin of the Younger Fill is the subject of considerable debate, and some scholars argue that it is simply the last stage in an intermittent process which began some two thousand years earlier in the Middle Bronze Age. Be that as it may, Vita-Finzi demonstrated that a dramatic geomorphological change took place at the end of classical antiquity.

There are two main theories about the formation of the Younger Fill. The first, proposed by Vita-Finzi, is that it was formed as a result of climatic deterioration, and that it provides us therefore with information on a major, but hitherto unsuspected, cause of the collapse of the Roman Empire. But no contemporary chroniclers reported marked changes in climate, and consequently it is difficult to accept this explanation without more evidence. The alternative theory is that the Younger Fill was formed as a direct result of the collapse of the classical agricultural system. Failure to

[2] Claudio Vita-Finzi, *The Mediterranean Valleys*, Cambridge 1969: see, however, J.M. Wagstaffe, 'Buried assumptions: some problems in the interpretation of the "Younger Fill" raised by recent data from Greece', *Journal of Archaeological Science* 8, 1981, 247-64.

Fig. 19 Recording a section of the Younger Fill in the Biferno Valley, Italy. The figure with the ranging rod is indicating where a sample dated by C14 to 700 ± 70 was found. (Photo: Graeme Barker)

repair terraces as the mass-market for olive oil and wine declined led to erosion as previously revetted soils were washed away. It is a familiar process; one sees it in many parts of the Mediterranean today, as farmers plough deeply into terraced hillsides, creating furrows at right angles to valley bottoms, down which the torrential winter rains carry soil at an alarming rate. The implications of this process in Late Antiquity are considerable. It would have led to the degradation of the hill slopes and to marked morphological changes in valleys and estuaries, with implications not only for farming but also for road networks, harbours and towns; the fate of Olympia was by no means unique, and at Rome we read of major flooding in 715-31.

The Younger Fill will be investigated in greater detail as we refine our understanding of late Roman ceramics, for this will enable us to date the alluvia more closely. Even so, Vita-Finzi's hypothesis has already illuminated an important aspect of the Dark Ages though, as he points out, his belief was far from new; it stemmed from G.P. Marsh's comments of 1859:

> The decay of these once flourishing [Mediterranean] countries is partly due to ... that class of geological causes whose action we can neither resist nor guide, and partly also to the direct violence of hostile human force; but it is, in a far greater proportion, either the result of man's ignorant disregard of the laws of nature, or an incidental consequence of war and ecclesiastical tyranny and misrule.[3]

Bryan Ward-Perkins has initiated a detailed study of Luni's position on the Ligurian coastline as alluvial deposition transformed its harbour and coastal cultivation. Similarly a short discussion by Clive Foss of the silting of the harbour of Ephesus shows how important this question is in the eastern Mediterranean. Clearly there is scope for extensive research in the future, and the last word on the Younger Fill has yet to be written.

The cities of mainland Greece appear to have fallen into decay in the late sixth century or in the period of serious unrest during the reign of Heraclius. The origins of their collapse probably lay in the later fourth or fifth century as various barbarian groups overran the peninsula en route for Constantinople or northern Italy. The onset of this 'age of barbarism', as it is termed by the excavators of Corinth, is just as evident there as at Carthage or Luni. There are signs of violence; a house north of the Peribolos of Apollo, for example, was destroyed by fire. The accepted view is that the wave of destruction which struck Corinth in the sixth century should be attributed to the Slavs, who arrived in Greece during the winter of 578-9. Similarly at Athens several hoards of small coins from the Agora are attributed to this period, as are many individual coin-losses of minimal value. One collection of four hundred coins was discovered in the burnt-out remains of a flour mill in the north-western suburb of the early Byzantine

---

[3] Quoted by Vita-Finzi, op. cit., 105.

city. Another appears to have come from a building next to the Tholos, destroyed by fire.[4]

The fire at Corinth and the hoards from Athens imply a brief cataclysmic episode, possibly in the 580s. Nevertheless excavations also demonstrate that both cities survived into the seventh century. By this stage, however, they had ceded most of their hinterlands to the Slavic tribes. The chroniclers Menander Protector and John of Ephesus may have over-emphasised the impact of the Slavic attacks, but there is little doubt that the entire pattern of settlement in Greece was undergoing change. The *Monemvasia Chronicle* notes shifts of population from Corinth to the island of Aegina, and from Argos to the Cyclades, and Sinclair Hood has postulated the existence at this date of island refuges all round the Greek mainland. Nevertheless it remains to be seen whether the new 'refuges' were the result of movements of population or simply the creation of new industries as traditional occupations declined.[5]

A consistent pattern, however, is emerging. Yugoslavia, like Italy, experienced change in the sixth century. I.A. Mirnik's assessment of the Yugoslavian coin-hoards emphasises the point: for the sixth century he lists 19 coin-hoards; for the seventh 4; for the eighth none.[6] The Slavs had effectively annexed the Balkans by 600. In contrast, the predominance of hoards dating from the reign of Heraclius in the Cyclades and Crete tallies with our information from the Aegean cities of Asia Minor. It also tallies with the hoards known from Cyprus, including the immensely rich Kyrenia treasure.

---

[4] Athens: D.M. Metcalf, 'The Slavonic threat to Greece circa 580: some evidence from Athens', *Hesperia* 31, 1962, 134-57; Corinth: Robert L. Scranton, *Corinth, Volume XVI; Medieval architecture in the central area of Corinth*, Princeton 1957, 6-34.

[5] P. Charanis, 'The Chronicle of Monemvasia and the question of Slavonic settlement in Greece', *Dumbarton Oaks Papers*, 5, 1950, 139-66; Sinclair Hood, 'Isles of refuge in the Early Byzantine period', *Annals of the British School at Athens* 65, 1970, 37-45.

[6] I.A. Mirnik, *Coin Hoards in Yugoslavia*, Oxford (B.A.R. International Series 95) 1981; note also Vladislav Popovic, 'Les temoins archéologiques des invasions Avaro-Slaves dans L'Illyricum Byzantin', *Mélanges de l'école française de Rome* 87, 1975, 445-504.

Clearly the hoards of Heraclius' reign are an expression of the overwhelming Sasanian invasions in the second decade of the seventh century, which threatened even the Greek islands.[7] In the words of Clive Foss:

> The Persian war may ... be seen as the first stage in the process which marked the end of Antiquity in Asia Minor. The Arabs continued the work ...[8]

Foss has assembled the archaeological evidence for the 'twenty cities' of Asia, originally listed by the tenth-century Emperor Constantine Porphyrogenitus in his *De Thematibus*. The cities include Ephesus, Miletus, Pergamum, Sardis and Smyrna, all the scenes of massive excavations over the course of the last century.[9] They confirm the illustrious role of these cities in the Early Byzantine period; indeed many of them must have been engaged in commerce with places like Vandal Carthage. But in the seventh century, claims Foss, 'the most important new evidence from archaeology is the revelation of destruction'.[10] In the period after the Sasanian war most of these cities became more or less deserted. The great city of Ephesus is a telling barometer of these changing times. In the fifth century many parts of the classical city were being rebuilt, and all the signs point to an immense mercantile wealth as late as 600. The best examples of this late flowering have been found in the excavations alongside the Embolos, the monumental street in the centre of Ephesus, where crowded dwellings have been uncovered. Nearly all of them were lavishly decorated in the fifth or early sixth century, and their courtyards were floored with marble or mosaics. Then, suddenly, in about 614, to judge from the coin evidence, these residential complexes were destroyed by fire. There has been much debate about the cataclysmic end of these quarters: was

---

[7] D.M. Metcalf, 'The Aegean coastlands under threat', *Annual of the British School at Athens* 57, 1962, 14-23.

[8] Clive Foss, 'The Persians in Asia Minor and the end of Antiquity', *English Historical Review* 90, 1975, 721-47, esp. 747.

[9] Clive Foss, 'Archaeology and the "Twenty Cities" of Byzantine Asia', *American Journal of Archaeology* 81, 1977, 469-86.

[10] Foss, op. cit. in note 8: 742.

there an earthquake, or were the houses sacked by the Persian army in 616, or was there a major fire which began by accident? One thing is clear, however: none of the dwellings was rebuilt.

The sheer grandeur of the fifth and sixth centuries in Ephesus can be seen in the remains of the great Justinianic church of St John. In architectural and artistic terms the chroniclers led us to believe St John was close to Sancta Sophia and San Vitale in magnificence. Its floor was covered with elaborately cut marble, and among the many paintings was one depicting Christ crowning Justinian and Theodora. No less remarkable are the many mausolea and chapels of the period centred around the grotto of the Seven Sleepers. These Early Christian funerary remains testify to the wealth of its citizens in death, complementing their lavishly decorated homes by the Embolos.

But the picture changed after the Persian sack in 616. A new city wall was constructed, enclosing less than a square kilometre, while a citadel was established on the hill of Ayasuluk overlooking Ephesus (Fig. 20). The city wall defended a little of the harbour, which was evidently silting up by this time. Urban life clearly was waning quite dramatically when the first Arab attack took place in 654-5. To meet this threat Ephesus became the capital of a military region, a theme, but its archaeology implies that it was little more than an administrative stronghold in the following centuries.[11] Foss concludes:

> The great changes took place in the Dark Ages ... Almost all the cities suffered a substantial decline; Smyrna alone may have formed an exception. In some instances, the reduction was drastic. Sardis, Pergamum, Miletus, Priene and Magnesia became small fortresses; Colossae disappeared, to be replaced by a fort high above the ancient site ... The cities reached their lowest point in the seventh and eighth centuries ... urban life, upon which the classical Mediterranean culture had been based, was virtually at an

[11] Clive Foss, *Ephesus after Antiquity. A late Antique, Byzantine and Turkish city*, Cambridge 1979.

Fig. 20 Ephesus. One restored column of the Temple of Artemis is in the foreground. In the background, the Mosque of Isa Bey and the hill of Ayasuluk with the Byzantine fortress. (Photo: Clive Foss)

end; one of the richest lands of classical civilisation was now dominated by villages and fortresses.[12]

Michael Hendy has corroborated this in his discussion of Early to Middle Byzantine coinage, and he quotes a ninth-century Arabic geographer:

In days of old cities were numerous in *Rum* (Anatolia) but now they have become few. Most of the districts are prosperous and pleasant and have each an extremely strong fortress, on account of the frequency of the raids which the fighters of the faith direct upon them. To each village appertains a castle where in time of flight they may take shelter.[13]

[12] Foss, op. cit. in note 9, 486.

[13] M.F. Hendy, 'Byzantium, 1081-1204: an economic reappraisal', *Transactions of the Royal Historical Society*, 5th series, 20, 1970, 31-52, especially 36.

Despite all this, the discovery of a wreck at Yassi Ada, off
the south-west coast of Turkey, dating to about 625, shows us
that a certain amount of seaborne trade continued. The boat,
which drew some 30 to 40 tonnes, belonged to one Georgios. It
was shipping nine hundred amphorae southwards along the
west coast of Asia Minor when it struck a reef and sank in 35
metres of water. The boat had a hold and a well-designed
galley at the stern. It is the finds associated with this ship that
are illuminating as far as we are concerned, for all the
evidence points to the continuing existence of a market-
economy in about 625, when it sank. Apart from the obvious
point that it was carrying a cargo of wine in mass-produced
containers (Fig. 21), we have the important assemblage of
kitchen wares from the galley. These include tablewares –
pitchers, jugs, plates and a cup – and storage amphorae.[14] There
were lamps and stone mortars as well as copper cauldrons. The
finest tableware was made of glass and was kept in a cupboard.
The same cupboard contained a large steelyard bearing the
name of Georgios and a smaller one with a set of silver-inlaid
weights. A group of coins, also found in the cupboard, consisted
of sixteen gold (Fig. 18) and more than fifty copper pieces. They
were probably in the master's safe-keeping for the duration of the
voyage, just as the Rhodian sea-laws of the time advised.

Georgios, it appears, was an entrepreneur in the last days of
the ancient economy. It is also evident from the equipment in
the galley that potters, metalworkers, glassworkers, mortar-
makers and the like were still marketing a range of more or
less standard products, as they had in earlier centuries.
Indeed Michael Metcalf uses coin-hoards to suggest that trade
persisted in the Aegean until the middle of the seventh
century. He draws attention to the coastal distribution of the
finds, as though merchants like Georgios were passing
between the last strongholds of the classical urban society.[15]
The end of the island economies, it appears, came during the
next twenty to thirty years. Excavations at ancient Carpasia
on the north coast of Cyprus have shown that the cathedral

[14] Frederick Van Doorninck, 'Byzantium, mistress of the sea: 330-641', in
George F. Bass (ed.), *A History of Seafaring*, London 1972, 133-58.
[15] Metcalf, op. cit. in note 7.

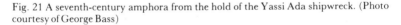

Fig. 21 A seventh-century amphora from the hold of the Yassi Ada shipwreck. (Photo courtesy of George Bass)

complex persisted until the middle of the century, protected along with the small harbour and a few other buildings by a newly constructed town wall. Economic decline, however, as well as Persian and later Arab raids had cumulative impact on even the island communities in the eastern Mediterranean. A great fortress was built at Paphos on the south-west coast of Cyprus early in the seventh century, but recent excavations suggest that even this bulwark with massive flanking towers had a short life (Fig. 22). Arab attacks along the coast decimated the population it was designed to protect. The chance discovery of a cave in the Kyrenia mountains, known as the Kornos cave, inhabited at this time, is a further reminder of turbulence.

Fig. 22 The seventh-century fort and later Crusader castle known as 'Saranda Kolones' at Paphos, Cyprus. (Photo courtesy Richard Anderson and A.H.S. Megaw)

Similarly the excavations at Emporio on the island of Chios found that one tower of the Justinianic fortress had been fired in the 660s. The scatter of coins in the debris points to the Arabs as the attackers, and chroniclers recount the invasions of Arab raiders on Chios as they made their way to attack Constantinople. The Arab raids, it seems, conclusively ended Early Byzantine trade, even on the modest scale we have suggested.[16] Indeed they delivered the coup de grâce to a system already so weakened that it was scarcely able to resist.

[16] Joan du Platt Taylor & A.H.S. Megaw, 'Excavations at Ayios Philon. The Ancient Carpasia', *Report of the Department of Antiquities of Cyprus* 1981, 209-50; A.H.S. Megaw, 'Excavations at "Saranda Kolones", Paphos, 1966-67 and 1970-71', *Report of the Department of Antiquities of Cyprus* 1971, 117-46; H.W. Catling & A.I. Dikigoropoulos, 'The Kornos Cave: an early Byzantine site in Cyprus', *Levant* 2, 1970, 37-62. The excavations at Emporio are only noted in J.M. Cook & J. Boardman, 'Archaeology in Greece, 1953', *Journal of Hellenic Studies* 74, 1954, 162-4, and in the *Supplement to the Journal of Hellenic Studies* 75, 1955, 20-3.

Byzantium and the Arabs

Justinian reimposed unified rule on the Mediterranean (Fig. 23). We have already mentioned the construction of fortresses and strategic hamlets in Italy to halt the Lombards and to meet whatever other crisis might emerge. More elaborate forts were constructed in Greece, such as the fortress outside the classical city of Isthmia in the Peloponnese or the important fortress at Emporio on Chios. These forts with their corner towers and bastions were designed to resist the violent assaults of fast-moving raiders. At the same time Justinian improved the efficiency of the navy, constructing new harbours like the one recently excavated by the German Archaeological Institute at Anthedon, on the coast of Thrace.[17] Justinian was also responsible for fortifying the ports of Asia Minor. The walls of Smyrna, for example, were refurbished and proved strong enough to withstand the Sasanian onslaught of 616.

Justinian's military works are most impressive in North Africa. Procopius lists the Emperor's works in his *Buildings,*

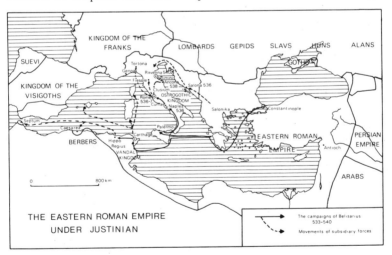

Fig. 23 The campaigns of the Emperor Justinian's armies

[17] H. Schläger, D.J. Blackman & J. Schäfer, 'Der Hafen von Anthedon mit Beiträgen zur Topographie und Geschichte der Stadt', *Archäologie Anzieger* 83, 1968, 21-98.

and Evagrius writes of them in his *Ecclesiastical History*. According to Evagrius, 'Justinian restored 150 towns in Africa; some he rebuilt completely; others, that were for the most part in ruins, he restored with even more magnificence'.[18] Evagrius, of course, was exaggerating, perhaps wildly, but the underlying point has been borne out by archaeologists over the past hundred years. The towns in question varied from Carthage, which enclosed some 390 hectares, to some scarcely two hectares in area. Without exception the Justinianic walls enclosed smaller areas than the earlier ones had done. For example, the Byzantine wall at Lepcis Magna originally enclosed 44 hectares, and even this was eventually reduced to 28; the Severan town covered no fewer than 130 hectares. At Sabratha the southern stretch of the Byzantine wall was erected through a part of the town that was already deserted. In some cases the scaling down of defences may have been simply to reduce expenditure; yet at the same time the most recent archaeological surveys of Libya leave little doubt that the population of North Africa was declining and that there were fewer people to defend.[19]

A century after Justinian the fate of the Empire as a Mediterranean unity was sealed. All the evidence suggests that the forts were ineffective opposition to the fast-moving raiders, who in some cases made pacts with dissident local groups. The Arab assault on North Africa began in 639, only seven years after the death of the Prophet. The conquest was made possible by desert tribesmen from Syria and Arabia who, under 'Amr ibn al-As, challenged the unpopular Byzantine administration of Egypt with an army of about 12,000 men. In 641 'Amr forced the Byzantine evacuation of the fertile Nile delta. Nubia was invaded in 641-2 and again ten years later, but here the Arabs could make no headway. Instead they turned on Cyrenaica. Richard Goodchild, after more than twenty years' research in Libya, concluded that the Arabs were able to break through the 'extraordinarily impressive' Byzantine defences in the Cyrenaican Jebel

[18] Quoted by Denys Pringle, *The Defence of Byzantine Africa from Justinian to the Arab Conquest*, Oxford (B.A.R. International Series 99) 1981, vol. i, 110.
[19] Ibid.: vol. i, 118-20.

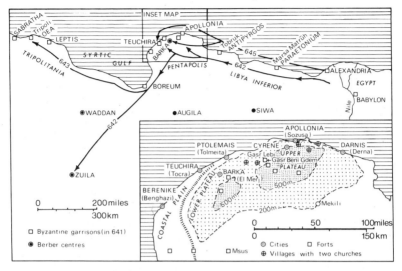

Fig. 24 The Arab invasion of Cyrenaica. (After Richard Goodchild)

because they were welcomed by the Copts (Fig. 24). The Copts hoped that the Moslems would prove powerful allies against their orthodox Christian enemies, though of course they were mistaken. In the end the Berber tribesmen of the pre-desert sided with the Arabs, and together they removed all the Christian communities in Cyrenaica. The Arabs rushed through the once-great province, and at Apollonia they began the systematic destruction of the palace and associated buildings of the Imperial adminstration. (The palace had sheltered for a short period no less a person than the future Empress Theodora who, as Procopius tells us, came to Libya Pentapolis as the mistress of its governor, Hekebolos.) Goodchild's excavations here showed that the Arabs had squatted in the building for a short time, and overturned the columns of all the city's churches during their stay. The recently excavated church at Berenice (modern Benghazi) shows the same signs of deliberate demolition.[20] Tripoli fell in

[20] Richard Goodchild, 'Byzantines, Berbers and Arabs in seventh-century Libya,' *Antiquity* 41, 1967, 115-24; J.A. Lloyd (ed.), *Excavations at Sidi Khrebish Benghazi (Berenice)*, vol. i (Supplements to Libya Antiqua V) London 1978, 173-94.

647, but the great province known as Africa (mostly modern Tunisia) resisted as long as the Byzantines remained masters of the sea. It was only later, when the Arabs deployed a navy, that Carthage, the Byzantine base, became vulnerable. In its last years the city had fallen into ruin, a mere shadow of its former grandeur. Even so it took three years before the city fell in 698. The site was abandoned and ultimately replaced by Tunis. The fall of Carthage opened the way to the coast of the Maghreb, and by 711 the entire coast of Africa, from Suez to the Straits of Gibraltar, was under Islamic control. The army then swept into Spain, and continued irresistably to Provence, while a splinter group passed through Aquitaine and advanced to the Loire. Its presence terrified the Merovingian community, and news of the invasion reached the historian Bede at distant Jarrow in northern England. At Poitiers,

Fig. 25 A decorated silver dish from the late seventh-century hoard found at Kyrenia, northern Cyprus. (Courtesy the British Museum)

however, the Moslems were halted in a battle, which was regularly celebrated by the Carolingian chroniclers of the ninth century. None the less by this time a new empire had been created, extending from Sind to Spain and including the southern shore of the Mediterranean.

The Dark Ages

Having achieved so much in such a short time, the conquerors seem to have run out of steam. Unlike the Vandals who prized the classical cities of North Africa, the Arabs simply abandoned them. As a result North Africa experienced a Dark Age which lasted until the tenth century, when Mediterranean and trans-Saharan trade revived and many new towns were developed.

In the eighth and early ninth centuries Byzantium was troubled by opponents from within as well as without. In the wake of its many defeats historians have identified a new patriotism within Byzantium which paradoxically led to further problems and internal divisions. To quote Peter Brown, the burning problem was how 'to adjust to the crevasse that had opened between their rich Late Antique past and an anxious present overshadowed by the armies of Islam'. The Byzantines turned from the images of Emperors to icons to find their miracles: an insular move which resulted in new internal divisions. Brown, like many scholars, has emphasised the decline of the cities as a key feature in the growth of Iconoclasm. It was a cult of one isolated city, Constantinople, and of an increasingly rural community.[21] Plagued by disputes, Byzantium passed into international oblivion for nearly two centuries, and (unexpected as this may be) its economic history will barely affect us again in this book.

We have surprisingly little archaeological information for the Mediterranean in the eighth or ninth centuries. All the classical towns were falling into ruin, as Foss has shown in Asia Minor. Even Otranto, Byzantium's only naval base of any substance in Italy, at the heel of the peninsula, has

[21] Peter Brown, 'A Dark Age crisis: aspects of the Iconoclastic controversy', *English History Review* 88, 1973, 1-34.

Fig. 26 Excavations at Otranto, southern Italy. (Photo: Demetrios Michaelides)

revealed very few structures of this era in a recent excavation, in sharp contrast to the wealth of finds from late ninth- to twelfth-century deposits (Fig. 26). Elsewhere in Italy Dark Age coinage emphasises this picture. Curious lead coins were found at Cosa in Tuscany and are identified as minted at Luni *c*. 600, while gold tremisses and solidi continued to be used in the duchy of Beneventum in central southern Italy long after gold had been found an impractical medium in Merovingia and Anglo-Saxon England. The coinage of Middle Byzantium, as Michael Hendy has shown, was a poor and confused shadow of the earlier and later systems.[22]

The state of Rome during the Dark Ages is intriguing. Like Byzantium, it continued to be not simply large, but very large,

[22] Lead coins: Luigi Tondo, 'Monete Medievali da Ansedonia (Grosseto)', *Archaeologia Medievale* 4, 1977: 300-5; south Italian Byzantine coins: Philip Grierson, 'Coinage and money in the Byzantine Empire, 498-*c*.1090', in *Moneta e Scambi nell' Alto Medioevo*, Settimane di Studio del Centro Italiano di Studi sull' Alto Medioevo, VIII, Spoleto 1961, 411-53; Hendy, op. cit. in note 13.

by local standards; yet the size of the artisan population is far from clear, and we must ask whether Rome reverted to being primarily the seat of church and state government (Fig. 27). Richard Krautheimer's recent profile of Rome emphasises the prevalence of monasteries within the decaying classical city, though none of these appears to have prospered until Stephen II and Hadrian I struck up an important relationship with the Carolingians. Whether these monasteries were

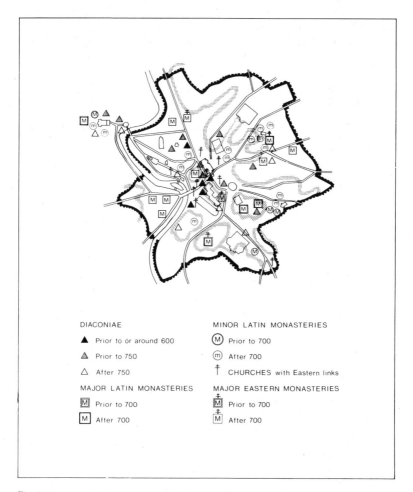

DIACONIAE

▲ Prior to or around 600

△ Prior to 750

△ After 750

MAJOR LATIN MONASTERIES

Ⓜ (boxed) Prior to 700

Ⓜ (boxed) After 700

MINOR LATIN MONASTERIES

Ⓜ Prior to 700

ⓜ After 700

† CHURCHES with Eastern links

MAJOR EASTERN MONASTERIES

Ⓜ (boxed, crossed) Prior to 700

Ⓜ (boxed, crossed) After 700

Fig. 27 Rome in the Dark Ages. (After Richard Krautheimer)

simply isolated communities within an otherwise depopulated townscape has yet to be investigated, for Krautheimer himself pays little attention to urban housing or population within the city.[23] The same questions can be posed at Lucca, Pavia and Ravenna, cities which many historians believe to have persisted unaffected by the gloom of the Dark Age recession. Were there simply royal villages and modest administrative centres situated within the once impressive streets of monumental buildings? Only excavations will answer the question. Pending such excavations, few would doubt that the case for urban collapse and a dramatic mercantile recession in Italy between the early seventh and mid-ninth centuries is a strong one.

In the later eighth or early ninth century the Mediterranean began to revive, but on a modest scale compared with the North Sea and the Baltic (according to new evidence). Apart from Venice, Italy as far south as Beneventum was drawn into a Carolingian orbit, and as a result looked northwards.[24] By contrast, the capture of Crete by the Arabs in the ninth century stimulated a regional network in the southern part of the Aegean. The discovery of a ninth-century Arab building close to Knossos on Crete with nine coins in its trampled floor adds a further dimension to the distribution of similar coins round the Greek mainland and the Cyclades. George Miles noted three of these Cretan copper coins in Athens, eight in Corinth and several from elsewhere on Crete itself and on neighbouring islands.[25] This is as yet tenuous evidence for a minor network, but it is worthy of further investigation. It also illuminates the growing Islamic desire to annexe the richer zones of the Mediterranean and introduce a new impetus to their slumped productivity. It was no coincidence that, as we shall see, the Moslems raided the rich parts of Sicily and Calabria first, and that they aimed for the rich monasteries of southern and central Italy.[26]

[23] Richard Krautheimer, *Rome: profile of a city 312-1308*, Princeton 1980, 89-108.

[24] Foss, op. cit. in note 9; for Otranto: D. Whitehouse & D. Michaelides, 'Scavi di emergenza a Otranto', *Archeologia Medievale* 6, 1979, 269-70.

[25] Peter Warren & George C. Miles, 'An Arab building at Knossos', *Annals of the British School at Athens* 67, 1972, 285-96.

[26] Nicola Cilento, *Italia Meridionale Longobarda*, Naples 1966, 175-98.

The archaeological evidence for the rural economy of the Dark Ages is still extremely slight. Nevertheless there are indications that the Arabs, Byzantines, Lombards and Slavs practised what were different variations of manorial economies, directed principally towards self-sufficiency. Some traditional industries continued, as the potter's kiln at Dhiorios on Cyprus, for example, illustrates.[27] Agricultural and industrial surpluses were translated into conspicuous wealth, such as fine places to worship or elegant jewellery, to reinforce the fragile political position of the elites. Between the reign of Heraclius and the Arab raids of the ninth century internal relations within the Mediterranean were reduced to an almost 'prehistoric' scale. Traders were few and far between. It is a startling contrast to what was happening in north-west and northern Europe at this time.

Conclusion

Archaeology is beginning to show that mercantile prosperity in the eastern Mediterranean outlasted that of the West by nearly a century. Italy and much of Greece fell to Lombards and Slavs soon after Justinian's death, but until the death of the Emperor Heraclius in 641 the eastern Mediterranean remained economically active. Nevertheless Byzantium was being eroded just as the Western Empire had been. The economy became focussed on the coastal fringes of Asia Minor, the Greek islands, Cyprus, and the North African littoral. The urban populations were dramatically reduced, partly perhaps as a result of the Great Plague of 542. In the countryside seventh-century farms are almost unknown to archaeologists, while the formation of riverine alluvium, the Younger Fill, may be a clue to radically changing agricultural practices.

The archaeological evidence, therefore, makes three points in relation to Pirenne's thesis. First, the Mediterranean did not switch from being a Roman lake to a Moslem one, as Pirenne proposed. Instead, before the advent of Islam, it had become divided into two major regions largely focussed upon Rome and Constantinople. When the former passed into the

[27] H.W. Catling, 'An early Byzantine pottery factory at Dhiorios in Cyprus', *Levant* 4, 1972, 1-82.

Dark Ages, Byzantium continued to generate trade in the east. After the eclipse of Byzantium, the 'lake' does not appear to have been the monopoly of any single power. Secondly, while the historical references to later sixth- and seventh-century Jewish and Syrian merchants in southern France, noted by Pirenne and his critics alike, are consistent with the view that some long-distance trade continued as late as Heraclius' reign, the archaeological evidence is firmly against the view of trade on a massive scale. Thirdly, we cannot doubt that in the seventh century Islam conquered an already decaying civilisation. Islamic expansion, like the Sasanian inroads a generation earlier, is a symptom of the deep-rooted social and economic decline of the Roman world, not a cause. The Arabs came, as the barbarians did to Britain and Gaul two centuries before, attracted by the prosperity. If they were conscious of Rome's collapse, they were probably as mystified by it as historians have been ever since.

Fig. 28 A Byzantine bronze buckle from Otranto. (Photo: David Whitehouse)

4. North Sea Trade and Commerce, 500-800

The fiercest debate about Pirenne's thesis has focused on the
nature of the early medieval economy in north-west Europe.
There are two crucial issues. First, Pirenne attributed the
character of the economy of the Carolingian era (the late
eighth and ninth centuries) to the closing down of the
Mediterranean economy by Islamic forces. In particular he
questioned the existence of towns in western Europe. In
Medieval Cities he wrote:

> An interesting question is whether or not cities existed in
> the midst of that essentially agricultural civilisation into
> which Western Europe had developed in the course of the
> ninth century. The answer depends on the meaning given
> to the word 'city'. If by it is meant a locality the population
> of which, instead of living by cultivating the soil, devotes
> itself to commercial activity, the answer will be 'No'. The
> answer will also be in the negative if we understand by 'city'
> a community endowed with legal entity and possessing
> laws and institutions peculiar to itself. On the other hand, if
> we think of a city as a centre of administration and as a
> fortress, it is clear that the Carolingian period knew nearly
> as many cities as the centuries which followed it must have
> known. That is merely a way of saying that the cities which
> were then to be found were without two of the fundamental
> attributes of the cities of the Middle Ages and of modern
> times – a middle-class population and a communal
> organisation.

Secondly, Pirenne questioned the existence of international
trade on any significant scale. On this highly controversial
issue Grierson has contributed a valuable insight:

The whole approach, that of accumulating evidence for the

Fig. 29 A gold tremissis of Madelinius (*c*.640 A.D.) minted and found at Dorestad (Courtesy the Dutch State Archaeological Service)

existence of trade instead of trying to form an overall picture of how and to what extent material goods changed ownership, is in itself profoundly misleading and can only result in conclusions that are far from the truth.

In the first part of this chapter, therefore, we shall consider the question of urban continuity in the light of numerous excavations in towns over the past twenty years. Then we shall review the archaeological evidence for Dark Age trade. We shall frame our discussion of this trade, however, in an anthropological rather than an historical perspective. This gives us a new insight into the rise of the Carolingians, using a source of evidence which has been ignored in the past.[1]

[1] Henri Pirenne, *Medieval Cities*, Princeton 1925, 56; Philip Grierson, 'Commerce in the Dark Ages: a critique of the evidence', *Transactions of the Royal Historical Society*, 5th series, 9, 1959, 123-40, especially 124.

The historical setting

When considering the economy of the Dark Ages it is important that we do not lose sight of its origins. Medieval historians turn back either to the fifth or to the seventh century when discussing the issue, and there they stop. Yet the political configurations of medieval Europe undeniably grew out of the migrations of the fourth and fifth centuries, and these migrations have much to do with the contacts that existed between the Romans and the 'Germanic' communities to the north and east. The Rhine was the axis of north European commerce in the later Iron Age, and the Romans simply built upon and extended pre-existing links. As a result the political institutions of the north Germans and south Scandinavians were modified by the commerce between the two very different communities. Only in the past decade has the intensity of these relations become clear through excavations in north Germany, Jutland and southern Sweden which reveal settlement plans implying marked social change linked to the increase in imported manufactured goods long noted in the accompanying cemeteries. Undoubtedly the stresses within the later Roman world were felt on the periphery, and we cannot overlook trade relations with Rome when we study the 'barbarian' migrations westwards into Romanised territories.[2] The scale of these mass-movements may have been exaggerated, but they reflect the gradual decay in the fourth century of the Rhineland as a major economic zone within the Empire. By the end of the century, two new communities were emerging: the kingdoms of the Ripuarian Franks on the middle Rhine and the Salian Franks in northern France. These Frankish territories were the first of the Germanic kingdoms to coalesce, as the political unity forged by the Romans out of a mosaic of Iron Age tribes in Germany and Gaul collapsed. The new kingdoms of the Franks developed, as we saw in Chapter 2, at the same time as those of the Visigoths in Aquitaine, the Burgundians and the

[2] Lotte Hedeager, 'A quantitative analysis of Roman imports in Europe north of the Limes (0-400 A.D.), and the question of Romano-Germanic exchange', *New Directions in Scandinavian Archaeology* 1, 1978, 191-216.

Alemans in other parts of the Western Empire.

The fortunes of the Franks changed dramatically under Clovis, who was crowned at the age of 16 in 481. Gregory of Tours tells us much about this charismatic leader in his *History of the Franks*, and we should remember that Clovis' reign coincided with that relatively stable period in the western Mediterranean when Odoacer and Theodoric were kings of Italy. Clovis was principally responsible for the expansion of the Frankish kingdom to embrace virtually all of northern France. He also captured most of Aquitaine, and as a result became a threat to Theodoric the Ostrogoth, who sent his general Ibbas to protect Provence against the Visigoths. The Goths, however, lost. When Clovis died in 511 he had formed a massive kingdom. As was customary with the Germanic kings, however, he divided his realm between his sons: there were four of them, and the massive kingdom disappeared. Of the sixth-century kings few stand out in a political world which, in the words of the Victorian historian Thomas Hodgkin, consisted of 'a wearisome succession of Chilperics and Childeberts ... '[3] Meanwhile, the Ripuarian Franks on the middle Rhine gradually added to their territory and formed a kingdom of the 'east lands' – Austrasia – while Francia in the west became Neustria – the 'new lands'.

Gregory's *History* depicts the gradual decay of Roman institutions and the concomitant fragmentation of the western provinces into a number of smaller territories, where aggressive leaders lived off the deteriorating Roman estates. Nineteenth-century archaeologists uncovered several such estates on the Loire and in Aquitaine. The discoveries seem to suggest that Roman institutions persisted, but in a considerably degraded form.[4] By the seventh century, however, the growth of a local nobility in each of the western kingdoms was undermining the central authority of the king. Hence, with the possible exception of King Dagobert of Neustria, there occurred a decline of central authority, which militated against the emergence of any polity able to combine

---

[3] Cited by Philip Dixon, *Barbarian Europe*, London 1976, 76.
[4] John Percival, *The Roman Villa*, London 1976, ch. 9.

the many diverse components. In the words of Einhard, the ·
biographer of Charlemagne, 'the king had nothing left but the
enjoyment of his title and satisfaction of sitting on his throne,
with his hair long and his beard trailing, acting the part of a
ruler'. The real power of the Frankish kingdoms in the later
seventh and eighth centuries passed to the *Maiores Domus* – the
Mayors of the Palace – the leading court officials.

The political situation was transformed in the late seventh
century when Pepin of Herstal, Duke of the Austrasians,
defeated the Mayor of the Neustrian Palace in battle, and
asserted the supremacy of the Austrasians over their western
neighbours. Pepin permitted the Neustrian king to retain his
throne, but he undertook campaigns against the Frisians, the
Bavarians and the Alemanni. His bastard son, Charles Martel
('Charles the Hammer'), assumed the same political mantle
when Pepin died in 714, and it was he who stopped the Arabs
at Poitiers in 732. Charles also extended his father's
annexation of Frisia and the territories to the east of the
Rhine, sometimes employing Anglo-Saxon missionaries to
pave the way for contacts with the pagans. In order to
maintain a fighting machine, Charles confiscated land and
redistributed it, perhaps to support a cavalry elite who might
be deployed rapidly to meet threats from the north, the east
or the south. But when he died in 741 his territory was divided: one of his sons, Carloman, took Austrasia and Alemannia,
and the other, Pepin the Short, Neustria and Burgundy. Six
years later Carloman retired to the monastery of Monte
Cassino and Pepin became the leader of the Franks. After a
further four years Pepin deposed Childeric III, the last heir of
Clovis, and was formally anointed king. Pepin campaigned
successfully in Italy against the Lombards on behalf of the
Pope, in Aquitaine against the Aquitanians and in Provence
against the last Islamic enclaves. By 768 he had established a
powerful reputation and a mighty kingdom. At his death
Francia was divided yet again, this time between his two sons
– Charles (Charlemagne, as he came to be known) and the
younger Carloman. The two brothers were at loggerheads
from the beginning, but in 771 Carloman died mysteriously
and his family fled to Lombardy. Charles seized control of
Francia and thereupon began an outstanding career, which

lasted 43 years. In the course of the next quarter-century, the political map of Europe was transformed beyond recognition. More significantly, the culture and economy of western Europe was also transformed. Such was its importance that the legacy of Charlemagne is usually referred to as the Carolingian Renaissance. It was a legacy that Pirenne regarded as the 'scaffolding of the Middle Ages'.

Urban decay

The nub of the debate about Pirenne's thesis seems to be the towns. Was there significant post-classical continuity of town life north of the Alps or not? If so, can we determine whether the functions of the town continued unaltered? All over Europe archaeologists and historians have devoted considerable energy to these questions. Indeed, to quote the eminent historian Edith Ennen, 'every swing of the pendulum in this controversy has provided an abundance of material ...'[5]

What abundance of material has emerged from two decades of unprecedented archaeological activity in the towns of western Europe? To begin with, it is now clear that many towns founded and developed during Roman times continued to be occupied until the sixth century. It is equally clear, however, that after the fourth century most of them experienced a dramatic change in their fortunes. From the mid-fourth century onwards few monumental buildings other than churches were built in Gallic towns, and virtually none was constructed in the towns of Roman Britain. Instead there is increasing archaeological evidence to show that decaying masonry buildings were either patched or demolished and replaced by timber structures.[6] For example, painstaking excavations at Wroxeter in Shropshire first revealed the vestigial remains of fifth-century timber long-halls in the old town centre. The traces of these buildings can only be detected by meticulous excavation, in which every stone on

---

[5] Edith Ennen, *The Medieval Town*, Amsterdam 1979, 17.
[6] Martin Biddle, 'The towns', in D.M. Wilson (ed.), *The Archaeology of Anglo-Saxon England*, London 1976, 99-150.

the site is plotted and thin occupation layers are removed in 5-10 centimetre spits. This kind of excavation, quite obviously, is only possible under research circumstances and is impractical for salvage excavations. As a result, we do not know how common such timber buildings were in later Roman France, for example, though excavations in many Roman towns in England have already produced traces of this kind.

Although the dying towns remained administrative and ecclesiastical centres, they no longer accommodated manufacturing industries as they had done in classical times. Shops and many of the industries characteristic of the Roman period had ceased to operate in Gaul by the fifth or sixth century. Moreover there was a marked decline in the variety of goods on offer after about 400. Indeed we have archaeological evidence from excavations of Frankish villages which suggests that crafts were now becoming organised at a domestic or village level of production.[7] The pattern of pottery production throughout Gaul and England reflects this change. In England, the Romano-British pottery industry ceased operations in the last decades of the fourth century and was replaced by village potters who produced limited ranges of hand-made wares. In Gaul the production of ,wheel-thrown wares in a variety of forms continued, but the scale of the industry and the numbers of active potters diminished. As a result, it looks as though one or two potters were able to meet the needs of entire regions in Merovingian and early Carolingian times. All the evidence, therefore, points to the scaling down of the artisan classes between the fourth and the seventh centuries, so that they had become small in number by the end of the Merovingian period.

But what of the eighth and ninth centuries? Colin Renfrew, writing on the nature of 'Dark Ages' in general, notes that one of their characteristics is a 'slow development [in the study of their archaeology], hampered both by [the tendency among historians to accept as evidence traditional narratives first set

---

[7] Pottery production in Austrasia is a good example of this: R. Koch, 'Absatzgebiete merowingerzeitlicher Töpferewen des nördlichen Nechagelsieter', *Jahrbuch für Schwabisch-Frankische Geschichte* 27, 1973, 31-43.

down in writing some centuries after the collapse] ... and by focussing on the larger and more obvious central place sites of the vanished state'.[8] This might have been written specifically of the early medieval period. For two decades urban archaeologists have doggedly searched for traces of seventh- to ninth-century occupation above Roman levels, simply to verify isolated historical references to the existence of an *urbs* or a *municipium*. Thwarted by the absence of early medieval deposits, there is the constant temptation to attribute tenth-century layers to the ninth century and so to recover at least something in the bid to prove urban continuity. In fact all these efforts provide us with an invaluable body of *negative* evidence against the continuity of towns after 600, and the case for discontinuity of urban life is very strong indeed. Of course the excavated areas are tiny percentages of the Roman or later medieval settlements; yet we cannot lightly dismiss the results. What then of the frequent references in the early medieval sources to the towns of Roman origin? Cologne, Paris, Tours, London, York, Winchester and many others are often mentioned, and this suggests that they were not abandoned. But we must appreciate what was in the minds of the chroniclers. One of the most vivid descriptions of a Dark Age 'city' is that of the ninth-century Irish monk, Cogitosus:

> What eloquence could sufficiently extol the beauty of this church and the innumerable wonders of what we may call its city? For 'city' is the proper word to use, since [Kildare] earns the title because of the multitudes who live there; it is a great metropolitan city. Within its outskirts, whose limits were laid out by St Brigid, no man need fear any mortal adversary or any gathering of enemies; it is the safest refuge among all the enclosed towns of the Irish.[9]

How large was this 'city'? In fact, Cogitosus was carried

---

[8] Colin Renfrew, 'Systems collapse as social transformation: catastrophe and anastrophe in Early State Societies', in Colin Renfew & Kenneth L. Cooke (eds), *Transformations: mathematical approaches to culture change*, London 1979, 463-506, especially 484.

[9] Quoted by Liam De Paor, 'The Viking towns of Ireland', in B. Almqvist & D. Greene (eds), *The Seventh Viking Congress*, Dundalk 1976, 29-37, especially 29.

away by rhetoric. It was a typical, near-circular, Irish monastery, barely 200 metres in diameter, but furnished with stone buildings. The monastery survives next to the main road from Cork to Dublin – a tiny medieval 'island' dwarfed by a modern housing estate. Cogitosus' city was probably a modest affair even by ninth-century standards and scarcely the type of settlement envisaged by either the Romans or by ourselves as a city. There is no doubt that monastic islands of this sort survived within the decaying remains of many Roman towns, as Henri Galinié has shown at Tours, for example.[10] The monasteries were the inheritors of Roman traditions, and they developed into the major foci of settlement in Carolingian Europe in the decades after the Benedictine synods at Aachen in 816 and 817. The St Gall Plan, compiled after the synods, probably gives us an ideal but not unfair impression of just such an 'island': a mixture of monumental, domestic and industrial buildings contained in a walled enclosure.[11]

Historians believe that the monasteries grew enormously during the course of the ninth century, with the greatest centres like Corbie, St Riquier and St Denys in northern France housing many thousands of monks and lay workers. Of course, how realistic these numbers are has yet to be properly evaluated.

Although many historical studies of the monasteries have been made, very few monastic sites have been examined by archaeologists in modern times. The current excavations at Reichenau on the edge of Lake Constance in southern Germany show the existence of the St Gall plan in real terms, while the latest campaign at the imperial abbey of Farfa (Fig. 30), just north of Rome, also reveals a carefully planned monastery. But only at San Vincenzo al Volturno (see p. 106) has it become clear that the eighth- and ninth-century monastery was essentially a closed economic environment, and not the quasi-urban community sometimes supposed by historians (Fig. 31).[12]

[10] Henri Galinié, 'Archéologie et topographie historique de Tours – IVème-XIème siècle', *Zeitschrift für Archäologie des Mittelalters* 6, 1978, 33-56.

[11] Walter Horn & Ernest Born, *The Plan of St Gall*, Berkeley 1979.

[12] We are grateful to Alfons Zettler for information on the current excavations at Reichenau. For Farfa see: Peter Donaldson, Charles

The only other 'islands' in the ruined town appear to have been the small palatial homes of the aristocracy. Again, although they are mentioned frequently in documents, we have only a vague impression of their character. This reinforces the point made about the monasteries. Aachen, Ingelheim and Nijmegen were the three greatest Carolingian palaces – palaces fit for an Emperor of the West: palaces where the administration of western Europe was handled. The Aachen palace-complex, imitating the architecture of the Romans, in reality illustrates the modest scale of Charlemagne's grandiose ambitions. By comparison with Theodoric's palace at Ravenna, Aachen was tiny. It was scarcely larger than the Byzantine governor's palace at

Fig. 30 A general view of the excavations at Farfa, Lazio in 1981. The ambulatory of the abbey can be seen (top left). A passageway in the centre leads from a probable gateway into the monastery, and a large room to the right of the passage has been uncovered. (Photo: David Whitehouse)

McClendon, David Whitehouse, 'Farfa – nota preliminare', *Archeologia Medievale* 6, 1979, 270-3; Farfa – seconda nota preliminare', *Archeologia Medievale* 8, 1981, 566-8; for San Vincenzo al Volturno see Richard Hodges, 'Excavations and survey at San Vincenzo al Volturno, Molise 1981', *Archeologia Medievale* 9, 1982, 299-310.

Fig. 31 A view of the South Church at San Vincenzo al Volturno, Molise, in 1982. Three undercrofts have been excavated beneath the nave of this early ninth-century church close to the entrance of the monastery. The nearest undercroft was a workshop; the central one was used as a stable, and the far one was probably a storeroom. (Photo: Richard Hodges)

Fig. 32 A model of the Carolingian and Ottonian palace at Ingelheim near Mainz. (Courtesy Römisch Germanisches Zentralmuseum, Mainz)

Apollonia in Tripolitania, excavated twenty years ago. The same is true of Ingelheim near Mainz, which was brought to light by Christian Rauch's excavations just before the First World War (Fig. 32). The compactness of these imperial palaces is also confirmed by the modern excavations at Schloss Broich on the river Ruhr. Schloss Broich was built in 883/4 and is in some ways a smaller version of Ingelheim. It covers a mere quarter of a hectare and is surrounded by a large stone wall. Inside there are ranges built up against the wall, and in the centre of the area there was a long, stone-built hall.[13] Nevertheless Schloss Broich, like Ingelheim and Aachen, was a palace in contemporary terms and it serves as a scale for the period. Like the great monasteries, the great palaces were modest, and they reflect the modest social and economic forces of the time.

It is safe to conclude that the hierarchy of markets had disappeared by about 600 in the Merovingian kingdoms. The historical data used to suggest the continuity of town life have distorted the true state of affairs. Instead there is archaeological evidence that monasteries and royal dwellings persisted in some 'classical' centres, but in real terms these were modest affairs. Neither of these classes of settlement maintained any large manufacturing industries, nor is there evidence of any additional urban populations. Industrial production, when it existed, was primarily a rural phenomenon, as we shall see in the case of the glass, pottery and quern industries of the Rhineland. In essence, Pirenne's analysis was close to the mark.

Trade routes and trading stations

Joachim Werner first drew attention to the north Italian and Coptic objects in cemeteries north of the Alps. Byzantine gold solidi which occur with the Coptic ladles, bowls and 'tea-pots' firmly date this transalpine commerce to between the very end of the fifth century and about 560 – the reigns of Theodoric

---

[13] Ingelheim: C.H.R. Rauch & J.H. Jacobi, *Die Ausgräbungen in der Königspfalz Ingelheim 1909-1914*, Mainz 1976; Schloss Broich: Gunther Binding, *Die spätkarolingische Burg Broich in Mülheim an der Ruhr*, Dusseldorf 1968.

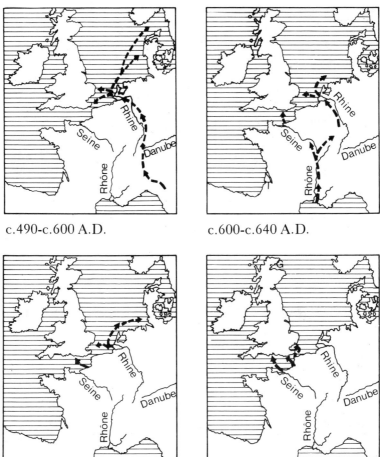

c.490-c.600 A.D.   c.600-c.640 A.D.

c.640-c.700 A.D.   c.700-c.830 A.D.

Fig. 33 The changing directions of long-distance trade in north-west Europe *c.*490-830 A.D.

and Justinian. Clusters of the finds have been mapped by Werner in north Switzerland, the central Rhineland and eastern and central Sweden. Outliers also occur in northern France and eastern England. During this last phase of Late Antiquity transalpine trading relations seem to have been established between the Ostrogoths and the new Frankish and

Scandinavian elites. Perhaps in return for these fine objects slaves were being exported southwards to fortify the brief reflationary period in the Mediterranean world described in Chapter 2.

Furthermore, at the same time ports in the Mediterranean were sending a few ships laden with eastern Mediterranean, Gaza and North African oils, wines and tableware to the Late Celtic Christian communities in Brittany and western Britain. Sherds of African Red Slip dishes similar to those described in the South Etruria Survey have been found at Tintagel, South Cadbury and other western British sites; at Garranes and at Clogher – two royal sites in Ireland; and at Dinas Powys in Wales. The Mediterranean amphorae have been found on many more sites besides and testify to a modest directional trade intended – we suppose – for royal and ecclesiastical strongholds anxious for imported commodities that afforded their owners prestige. What was traded in return remains obscure, but the ubiquity of these Late Roman Mediterranean imports is striking.

The sharp decline in the Mediterranean economy monitored in and around Carthage and Rome also resulted in the closing of trade-routes to the north (cf. Chapter 2). From the mid to late sixth century imports from the Mediterranean are rare in northern contexts; those that occur, as in early seventh-century Kent, can be assumed to be heirlooms or gifts passed from one generation to the next and ultimately interred.

Briefly at the turn of the sixth century the territory of Provence appears to have acted as the intermediary between north and south, but what passed this way, other than coins, is difficult to say. Certainly for some thirty to forty years after about 580 gold solidi minted in Provence are prominent finds in the coin hoards found at St Martin's, Canterbury, Escharen in Holland and Sutton Hoo in Suffolk. But the prominence of Provence evidently began to wane after about 630 when king Dagobert rose to power, and it may be no co-incidence that the Provençal coins after this time were rapidly devalued, and that they tend subsequently not to occur in central or northern French hoards in any significant number. From Dagobert's time, however, the nascent

Frankish mints from Bordeaux to Cologne and from Dijon to Amiens were also devaluing their coins ahead – or very slightly ahead – of the Provençal devaluation. All the evidence points to Provence as a short-lived acquirer of gold which was circulated for a decade or two in the form of currency, giving European prominence to the kingdom. (This may coincide with the very end of Early Byzantine trade in the eastern Mediterranean, to which we drew attention in Chapter 3.) This ceased, however, early in the seventh century. With it ceased the north-south contact which had begun more than a thousand years earlier, when Greeks and Etruscans traded with the Celts. The regional circulations of the devalued mid-seventh-century Frankish coins give a slight glimpse of the economic formation of Merovingia isolated from the Mediterranean – a transition that quite evidently happened before the Moslems overran the African coast and invaded Spain.[14]

While it is possible to trace the patterns of traded goods over substantial distances, it is another matter to explain the motives behind the trade. This is the principal reservation that historians have about archaeological evidence. But we have already noted that the motives for trade are no clearer in the isolated contemporary references to merchants. With this problem in mind archaeologists have sought anthropological and geographical assistance to evaluate the patterns of traded goods. First, if we adopt an evolutionary perspective of past social systems, we have to recognise that the early medieval kingdoms of western Europe may be defined as complex chiefdoms or incipient states. The economic correlates of such systems are not competitive markets. Instead the elites within these kinds of society foster administered markets in which the artisan classes are small and are usually affiliated to the elite. In such socio-economic systems the elites control the movements of valuable commodities. But as the elites are still governed by their kin-relations, they use luxury commodities

[14] Sixth and seventh-century trade and trade-routes are discussed in Richard Hodges, *Dark Age Economics*, London 1982, 29-39; see also Joachim Werner, 'Fernhandel und Naturalwirtschaft in östlichen Merowingerreich nach archäologischen und numismatischen Zeugnissen'. *Bericht der Romische-Germanischen Kommission* 42, 1961, 307-46.

to reinforce their position within the community. Prestigious goods are given as gifts in the form of bride-payments, tribute or taxation. Fine garments or jewellery are worn at public occasions to emphasise rank, and similar commodities may be destroyed ritually at funerals to indicate the wealth they enjoyed. In short, status equates to power; but, of course, as far as the individual is concerned power in these circumstances is a brittle commodity.

The most effective means of enhancing chiefly status is to establish a trade partnership with another leader who can offer prestigious commodities in exchange for goods raised by taxation. Trade partnerships of this kind are of signal importance for developing economies for they offer a possibility of swiftly accelerating the political position of the leader. In archaeological terms we can detect the emergence of trade partnerships when concentrated distributions of imported goods occur at some distance from their source. Distance, it should be noted, is less critical in such pre-market contexts where social value of the imported goods outweighs, or is bound up with, their economic value. Supply-and-demand factors which characterise market economies are subsumed to some degree in these pre-state societies.

As the volume of trade increases between the trade partners, kings or chiefs inevitably are forced to confine the commerce to specific trading places. If they do not, the commodities may be siphoned off to subjects who can afford such things, and the initial purpose of the exchange system will be defeated. Thus in many complex pre-market societies there are administered trading settlements that might appear to be colonies because they are mostly inhabited by alien merchants, and yet in terms of jurisdiction they are urban communities belonging to the native elite. Historians know such sites as emporia; geographers call them gateway communities; some anthropologists have referred to them confusingly as ports-of-trade. Without doubt they are one of the hallmarks of a complex pre-market economy and a complex pre-state society. Their social fabric is markedly different from states, where there is a political elite reinforced by military and bureaucratic force rather than its kin relations within society. Inter-regional market-places do not exist in pre-state societies, and the mode of production and distribution is far simpler and centrally organised. As will be apparent, Merovingian and Carolingian Europe falls readily into this definition, though we must remember that all the territories of early medieval Europe were evolving at a dramatic pace and that their character could alter almost between one generation and the next.[15]

The two principal Merovingian kingdoms, Neustria and Austrasia, founded trading sites giving access to the North Sea in the early seventh century. Numismatic and historical evidence points to the creation of a Neustrian settlement at Quentovic, south of Boulogne, and to a probable Austrasian settlement at Dorestad near Utrecht, in Holland. The precise location of Quentovic remains unknown, but it is thought to lie near the mouth of the river Canche near Etaples. A mass of historical evidence points to its economic importance until the mid-ninth century. Dorestad, by contrast, has been the scene of an enormous archaeological project directed by Professor W.A. van Es for the Dutch State Archaeological Service. It was situated at the junction of the rivers Rhine and Lek, and over the course of two centuries it grew to occupy more than 200 hectares. Another early seventh-century trading site has been located at Ipswich in East Anglia – presumably a base for the Wuffingas dynasty, who were buried at nearby Sutton Hoo. At this date Dorestad may have been the port from which traders set off for Ipswich and, possibly, Scandinavia. Meanwhile the Quentovic traders seem to have crossed to the short-lived site at or near Sarre, a village close to the (now silted-up) Wantsum Channel in Kent.

The growing body of evidence from seventh-century trading sites reveals that the trading networks were far from haphazard affairs. Their development owed much to the settled conditions that began to prevail after several centuries of migration and political upheaval. The introduction of silver coins in the 670s and 680s after a century of high-value gold coins in the Merovingian kingdoms fits this picture. Pirenne

[15] Hodges, op. cit. in note 14: ch. 1; see also Carol A. Smith, 'Exchange systems and the spatial distribution of elites: the organisation of statification in agrarian societies', in Carol A. Smith (ed.), *Regional Analysis*, vol. ii, London 1976, 309-74.

regarded this transformation as a sign of economic deterioration, but it may well reflect a growing commerce and the need for a smaller, serviceable currency. The growth of Quentovic and Dorestad at the same time points to a policy of trading goods manufactured in traditional Roman ways (such as wheel-thrown pots, glasses, corn-grinding quern stones and hones) to kingdoms where production was less sophisticated. In return raw materials like wool, hides or slaves could be acquired. Several historical passages illuminate these transactions and suggest that the trade was first agreed by treaties between particular kings or their agents. The late-eighth-century letters between Offa and Charlemagne are the most revealing examples of trade established by treaty.

Some historians might regard such arrangements as exploitative, but it would be wrong to infer any kind of primitive imperialism on the part of the Merovingian and Carolingian kings. The goods they traded sustained the arguably affluent economies of the Anglo-Saxons and Scandinavians. If, however, the traders had dealt directly with farmers in less controlled circumstances, they might easily have undermined the social status of the native kings. Hence, as the Merovingians and then the Carolingians inclined towards increasing commerce with their neighbours, it paid the Anglo-Saxon and Scandinavian kings to watch diligently over the long-distance trade and to contain the activities as far as was feasible.[16]

This socio-political rationale explains the concentrations of seventh-century objects at Dorestad and Ipswich, but we must bear in mind a further dimension. Strangely, while the Merovingian community appears to have preserved many aspects of Roman manufacturing, boat-building seems to have reverted to its earlier Celtic or Germanic traditions. The notable difference was that the 'Germanic' boats lacked keels to support strong masts for sails. Instead their boats were propelled by man power, with only moderate assistance from small sails set in keel-planks. The well-preserved boat discovered at Utrecht, dating to about 800, is a good illustration of this. Like the boats illustrated on coins minted

[16] Hodges, op. cit. in note 14, 47-86.

in the ninth century at Dorestad (Fig. 63), the Utrecht boat required at least twenty-four rowers. Once these were accommodated within the vessel there was scarcely any room for bulky cargoes. This state of affairs appears to have changed very slowly. The construction of deep-draughted boats with keels designed to take sails only appeared in north-west Europe at the turn of the millennium. The significance of this is considerable. Every trading venture – every transaction – involved not just the merchant and three or four sailors, as was the case in Roman times or even in the contemporary Byzantine world. Instead as many as two dozen men accompanied each trip. Their presence naturally restricted the cargo space. In other words, ten continental traders visiting Ipswich involved as many as 250 men. Moreover we can count on the traders to have brought their own cooking equipment when travelling to more primitive societies in which mass-produced goods were not available.

We must also remember that trading in these circumstances was often a long-drawn-out affair: the mercantile community had to be fed over long periods and satisfactorily accommodated. As a result, a small native population was needed for these specialist tasks, and very soon a modest seasonal community developed with its roots embedded in the trade-treaty arrangements between kings each summer season.[17]

The startling growth of the trading settlements had become apparent by the second quarter of the eighth century. Hamwih (Saxon Southampton) appears to have been founded in about 700 to control southern and central English commerce (Fig. 34). By the second quarter of the century Hamwih had become a 46-hectare settlement with a gridded street system. The imported pottery from rubbish pits points to its numerous trading relations with different centres in northern France, though most of the traders probably passed through the toll-station at Quentovic. It is also clear that Dorestad was growing at a staggering speed. Its excavator has estimated that it reached about 50 hectares by about 800. The evolution of Middle Saxon Ipswich follows a similar pattern, with an outlier

[17] Ibid., 94-100.

of the emporium being established on the south bank of the river Gipping at an early point in its history. In comparison with later medieval towns these Dark Ages sites may not seem unduly large, but we have to compare their size with the palaces and monasteries described above and with villages and hamlets, the only other settlements in existence at this time. It is unlikely that any of the latter exceeded 2-4 hectares anywhere in north-western Europe.

The Anglo-Saxon emporia show signs of deliberate planning, as though the kings involved in the trade had

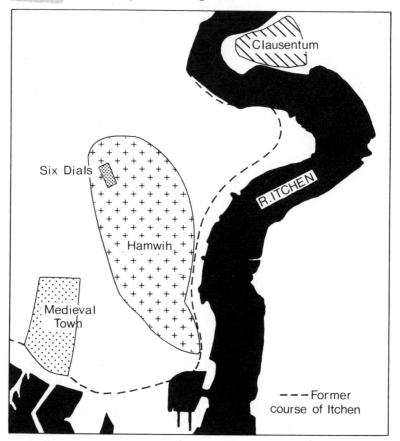

Fig. 34 A sketch-plan of the Middle Saxon emporium of Hamwih, Saxon Southampton

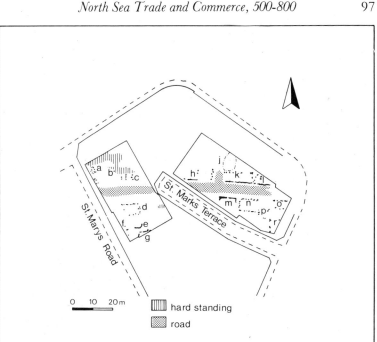

Fig. 35 A sketch plan of the Six Dials' site recently excavated in Hamwih. It shows the buildings aligned alongside the gravel road found in this northern sector of the emporium. (After *Current Archaeology*)

specified exactly where roads and buildings should be put. This is clearest at the Six Dials site in Southampton, where a network of roads and a boundary ditch have been uncovered (Fig. 35). On either side of the road are lines of buildings, and behind these are ancillary structures, wells and rubbish pits. The rubbish in these pits, like the rubbish buried in Dorestad and Ipswich, shows that the community was well fed on livestock, presumably from surrounding estates. The debris also indicates the range of crafts practised within these newly-established communities, which were not to be found elsewhere. These craftsmen serviced the aristocracy and on some occasions the farmers who lived within the immediate catchments of the ports. Mass-produced pots were made in Hamwih. There are signs of glass-working, bone-working was commonly practised, and it is likely that fine jewellery and the minting of coins also

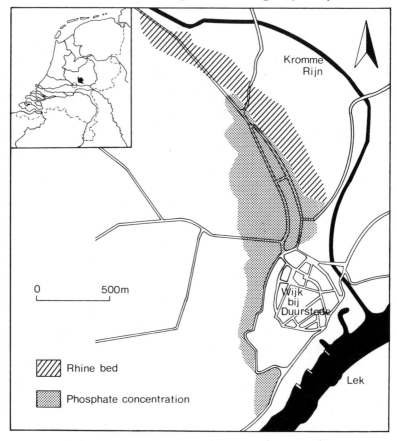

Fig. 36 The location and extent of Dorestad. (After W.A. van Es and W.J. Verwers)

took place. The planning of the settlements and their growth as industrial centres presents a new dimension in the debate on Dark Age trade. Until the middle of the eighth century most of this intense activity seems to have been confined to commercial relations between Austrasia and Frisia and East Anglia on the one hand, and between Neustria and southern England on the other. But, as rapidly as this trade developed, so it seems to have declined. After about 750 there was an inexplicable hiatus in cross-Channel relations, which prevailed until about 790.

After this a new boom in economic activity took place in the

Fig. 37 The piles for the plank walkways into the river Rhine at Dorestad. (Courtesy the Dutch State Archaeological Service)

decade before the end of the eighth century. To begin with, Dorestad seems to have reached its greatest size between about 780-790 and about 830 (Fig. 36). Merchant's buildings stretched along the banks of the rivers Lek and Rhine obscuring the inner native village which, it is believed, was the original nucleus of the site. Excavations in the former river bed of the Rhine have shown that plank walkways were constructed out into the river leading from each merchant's building. Dendrochronology shows that these walkways, against which boats were tied, were being replaced regularly, as well as extended (Fig. 37). By the end of the eighth century Dorestad was handling exclusively the products of the Middle Rhineland industries.

Wine was one major commodity which passed via Dorestad. Most of it was probably from vineyards around and to the south of Mainz – close to the imperial estates at Ingelheim. It seems that the Rhenish vintages were sent northwards in casks made from local timber. At Dorestad some were transferred to earthenware amphorae. Old wine barrels have been discovered in Dorestad, re-used as timber linings for wells dug in the soft sand on which the settlement developed. The amphorae, together with many different types of tablewares, were made in large pottery-producing villages in the Vorgebirge Hills west of Cologne and Bonn. It is believed that, as in the Roman period, glass vessels were made in the same region, though no evidence of the medieval industries has yet come to light. Early medieval glasshouses, however, are known from the hills around Trier, and it is likely that these products would have been transported up the river to Moselle and thence by the Rhine to Dorestad. In the Eifel mountains to the south of Bonn the quern-quarries were opened in the seventh century. These lava querns were greatly favoured for grinding corn in many parts of western Europe, and it appears that some were finished off in Dorestad. The 'blank' forms of others were sent on to Ipswich or Haithabu in north Germany, where chips from the finishing process have also come to light.[18]

Dorestad must have been the base of the celebrated Frisian traders. The Frisians were frequently described by contemporary monks, and a short poem even emphasises their romantic journeys around the Dark Age western world. They were without doubt the great entrepreneurs of the Carolingian period, acting as intermediaries between the Rhenish courts and the territories with which they were often at loggerheads. Moreover, as with the later Dutch sailors, the Frisians were evidently prepared to brave the seas and to undertake substantial voyages. Even so there is some historical exaggeration of the Frisian dominance of the North Sea, and whether these traders really monopolised the continental trade with England, for example, can be seriously questioned.[19]

It seems obvious that if we trace the distribution of the products that the Frisians were handling (and using) in Dorestad we can form an impression of the areas in which

[18] W.A. van Es & W.J.H. Verwers, *Excavations at Dorestad 1; The harbour: Hoogstraat 1*, Amersfoort 1980.

[19] Hodges, op. cit. in note 14: 87-94; see also Dirk Jellema, 'Frisian trade in the Dark Ages', *Speculum* 30, 1955, 15-36.

they were operating. What becomes immediately clear from this analysis is that the pattern of Rhenish finds is strongly concentrated along the North Sea coastline from Dorestad to Jutland. Only minor concentrations of the products occur in eastern England and in Sweden. The majority of imported items found in Southampton and Ipswich stems from northern France or Flanders. Then, again, the majority of the traded products around the Baltic Sea, with the exception of Jutland, originates from several different parts of the Baltic coastline, as well as from the east, as we shall see. There is good reason, therefore, not to exaggerate the overall importance of the Frisians, though the scale of Dorestad attests their great mercantile activity in some directions.[20]

To sum up, by 800 many thousands of people were directly or indirectly involved in a highly structured set of exchange networks. Indeed commerce had developed to resemble the pattern of later pre-Roman trading systems whereby the Roman Empire had acquired minerals, wool and slaves in return for finished manufactured goods. At the same time, until 800 all the evidence points to an economy primarily directed by the elites: kings, the aristocracy and the church; there were, of course, small and occasional rural markets for exchanging local produce, but these were not essential to the operation of the economy as a whole. The structure of the economy had changed radically from Roman times. It had begun to do so as early as the later fifth or sixth century north of the Alps, and for these reasons there inevitably occurred the developments which Pirenne perceived in outline. Yet, although so far we have given Pirenne's thesis a fresh perspective by adding an archaeological scale (with the assistance of an anthropological model) to the imprecision of history, it is time to determine whether this growth in the scale of commerce between the various Dark Age kingdoms was sufficient to provide the financial basis for Charlemagne's cultural and economic aspirations. This is the key question underlining Pirenne's thesis.

[20] Richard Hodges, *The Hamwih pottery: the local and imported wares from thirty years' excavations at Middle Saxon Southampton and their European context*, London 1981, 93-4.

5. Charlemagne and the Viking Connection

> Beneath this tomb lies the body of Charles the great and orthodox emperor, who nobly extended the kingdom of the Franks, and reigned prosperously for 47 years. He died, in his seventies in the year 814 ...[1]

The simple coffin in the Aachen palace-complex reveals the paradox of Charlemagne's career. In his first thirty years as king of Francia he enlarged his kingdom to include the Pyrenees, northern and central Italy, parts of Bavaria and most of northern Germany (Fig. 39). When he was crowned Emperor of the West on Christmas Day 800 he had achieved an almost unimaginable success, after which he inclined more and more towards the image of patron of the western Church, seeking to increase its status. At the same time he propagated a new spiritualism from his courts. This was the beginning of the Carolingian Renaissance – a cultural revolution that was dynamic for one generation, and remembered for at least another two. But the wars did not cease, and the untimely death of Charlemagne's elder sons meant that instead of being divided into three shares, the Empire was left to Louis, King of Aquitaine, as one massive entity.

Soon after his father's death Louis was persuaded to acknowledge his son Lothar as sole heir to his title, removing any immediate threat to the concept of the Empire. At the same time the Aachen synods of 816 and 817 called for a single, universally binding code of monastic rules to replace the many rules that had prevailed during previous centuries. These reforming synods accelerated the cultural revolution and created a need for new monasteries and, concomitantly, new art forms. Louis' court fostered the monumental redesigning of the monasteries, often at its own expense, and

---

[1] Cited by Philip Dixon, *Barbarian Europe*, London 1976, 106.

Fig. 38 An imitation dinar minted by King Offa of Mercia. (Courtesy the British Museum)

at the same time it created the milieu for craftsmen to make new church ornaments and prepare new copies of sacred texts and other works. So until about 830 the Carolingian courts were at the centre of this Renaissance fervour, and the rest of the western world took its lead from the court artists.

This phase of Imperial order was dramatically terminated soon after 828 when Louis bowed to the wishes of his second wife, Judith, and permitted her son Charles to have a share in the division of the Empire. Louis' elder sons challenged their father, and for fifteen years civil war engulfed the Carolingians, fatally preoccupying the aristocracy. During the mid 830s Scandinavian raiders began to appear regularly along the Carolingian and Anglo-Saxon coastlines, plundering settlements close to the sea. At the same time Saracens from the Maghreb began to attack Sicily as well as coastal centres in Byzantine, Beneventan and Papal parts of southern Italy. By 830 Charlemagne's imperial and cultural legacies were severely threatened. A mere ten years later the western world was in a state of turmoil, comparable in some respects to the century following Valens' death at Adrianople.

The finances of the Carolingian Renaissance

Charlemagne and his son Louis clearly promoted and paid for the Carolingian Renaissance. The revenues from many of their estates were invested in their great projects. David Herlihy has calculated that church lands over western

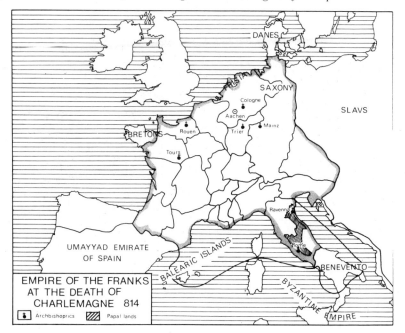

Fig. 39 The extent of Charlemagne's empire and influence in 814

Christendom as a whole tripled in area between 751 and 825, rising from 10 per cent to over 30 per cent of all the land under cultivation. This assembling of land led many great monastic houses to consider more efficient agrarian policies. Thus St Gall in Bavaria tried to group its dispersed estates into one large unit, while others like Bobbio and Farfa, for instance, made surveys of their property.[2] A clear emphasis was now put upon landed wealth as an expression of power. But was this wealth sufficient to finance the enormous building developments arising from the reforms demanded at the Aachen synods of 816/17? Excavations at numerous churches in West Germany over the past twenty years have indicated the staggering scale on which later Merovingian churches were being rebuilt. Cologne Cathedral, for example,

[2] David Herlihy, 'Church property on the European Continent, 701-1200', *Speculum* 36, 1961, 81-105.

Fig. 40 'Einhard's church' at Steinbach bei Michelstatt, West Germany

was entirely remodelled and in effect became a great church rather than a chapel, as it had been in Merovingian times. Einhard's church at Steinbach is a classic example of the ambitious new scale on which ecclesiastical architecture was being conceived (Fig. 40). The St Gall plan of an ideal monastery was drawn up soon after the synods of 816/17, and although it was evidently a scheme rather than a working design, it does seem to have influenced the form of fundamental changes at Reichenau, to judge from recent excavations there.[3] Similarly, the Imperial abbey at Farfa north of Rome was reconstructed on an ambitious scale including a large square room behind a substantial tower – possibly all part of the guests' quarters. Several of the ninth-century monasteries of Rome benefited from the close ties created between the Carolingians and the Popes. Again, a number of churches were enlarged, while others exhibit new wall-paintings or elaborate marble pavements harking back to later classical times. San Clemente was redecorated, while S. Prassede is a fine example wholly of this time. At SS. Quattro Coronati a massive new nave was constructed as well as a gateway tower. Archaeology,

[3] Information from Dr Alfons Zettler.

however, cautions us to be wary of over-emphasising the financial implications of these spectacular new buildings. In most cases the brick and marble could be found readily among ruins of the Roman period. Thus a classical temple was dismantled near Capua to provide the columns for the new cloister at San Vincenzo al Volturno in Molise, Central Italy. Louis the Pious provided the manpower to transport the columns up the Volturno valley. The new *opus sectile* pavements in San Vincenzo employed smashed or cut marbles which could also be found on classical sites. The only real 'expense' was labour. It seems likely that this could have been met by the monasteries themselves because many housed in excess of a hundred monks, and some like Tours claimed – not very convincingly – to house thousands.[4]

It is becoming clear from initial archaeological investigations that the countryside was under-populated (i.e., the population was much smaller than in late Roman or later medieval times). As a result regional economies were under-developed. Field surveys in the Middle Rhineland and in various parts of Italy have begun to emphasise the modest scale of rural settlement at this time.[5] There is, in fact, much to suggest that peasants had a comparatively high level of nutrition from maintaining mixed farming regimes in this pre-market environment, as opposed to producing cash crops of one form or another. The manufacture of pots, glasses, querns, metalwork and other archaeologically detectable products indicates that small-scale, quasi-industrial establishments existed perhaps in important monasteries and centres of authority. Equally the distribution of these goods was probably controlled by abbots or members of the aristocracy. The concept of the market-place had not died altogether, but its full re-establishment posed a formidable task for the Carolingian

[4] Farfa: Peter Donaldson, Charles McClendon, David Whitehouse, 'Farfa – nota preliminare', *Archeologia Medievale* 6, 1979, 270-3; 'Farfa – seconda nota preliminare', *Archeologia Medievale* 8, 1981, 566-8; San Vincenzo al Volturno: Richard Hodges, 'Excavations and survey at San Vincenzo al Volturno, Molise, 1981', *Archeologia Medievale* 9, 1982, 299-310.

[5] Walter Janssen, 'Some major aspects of Frankish trade and medieval settlement in the Rhineland', in P.H. Sawyer (ed.), *Medieval Settlement: continuity or change*, London 1976: 41-60; Hodges, op. cit. in note 4.

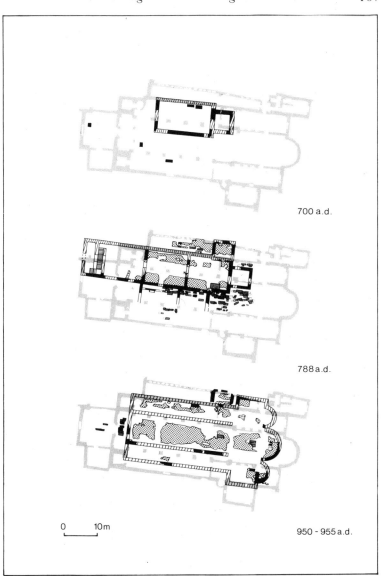

700 a.d.

788 a.d.

0   10m

950 - 955 a.d.

Fig. 41 The sequence of early medieval churches beneath the cathedral at Niedermünster, West Germany. (After Klaus Schwartz)

government. When asked recently to comment on the Carolingian economy, Georges Duby replied:

> Couldn't the economic historians, as their contemporaries obviously did, consider the great demesnes, the area of lordly rule, centering on the castle or the monastery, as self-sufficient families, as places of redistribution between a paternal force and all the satellite familial networks? At a higher level, the State manifested a similar structure. I have said of the Carolingian Empire [that] it was a village chieftaincy with universal dimensions. I could have demonstrated, perhaps more justifiably, that it was like a large family, gathered around one father ...'[6]

Initially the Carolingian Renaissance may have been fostered by accumulated wealth derived from the amassing of property. But whether this could be sustained over all the Empire remains in doubt. In addition, the Imperial patronage of the Church at the expense of the aristocracy may conceal one purpose intended for the monasteries, namely to be the spiritual means of binding this set of disparate territories together. Archaeology, however, is beginning to reveal evidence which contradicts the view that the Renaissance was sponsored by a gradual accumulation of wealth. In so doing it challenges the perspective Pirenne introduced to us of a gradually evolving feudal economy. It now suggests that along with the sudden and massive period of rebuilding there are also signs of sudden and massive economic expansion.

The first two features of this expansion run counter to Pirenne's belief in the gradual evolution of North Sea commerce alongside the formation of the great regional estates. First, it is apparent from recent excavations at Dorestad that this great emporium experienced an explosive increase in activity between the 780s and 820s. Evidently, Dorestad was expanding in response to the increased demand for specialised goods by the Imperial courts in the Middle Rhineland. The archaeological debris at Dorestad reflects the

[6] Georges Duby in 'Symposium: economic anthropology and history: the work of Karl Polanyi', *Research in Economic Anthropology* 4, 1981, 58-60.

Fig. 42 A silver denier of Louis the Pious from Dorestad. (Courtesy the Dutch State Archaeological Service)

strong Rhenish character of the emporium, in marked contrast to Ipswich and Hamwih where traders from a large number of widely separated centres in northern France and Belgium were present. Trade between Neustria and the Anglo-Saxon kingdoms was probably at its peak between about 790 and 830; yet comparatively little commerce passed between Dorestad and Ipswich, for example. Instead the massive enlargement of Dorestad at this time reflects commerce with Frisian and Scandinavian communities to the north of the Rhine. The Carolingian courts, it seems, were seeking commodities from the north which they themselves could not obtain, and so the Frisian entrepreneurs gained a vital role in the interchange.[7]

The second feature we must note is Charlemagne's reforms of the Carolingian coinage, which took place between 793 and 794. These reforms were followed by a series of edicts (issued by Charlemagne and Louis) urging the populace to use coin as the medium of exchange (Fig. 42). But the more important

[7] Reviewed in Richard Hodges, *Dark Age Economics*, London 1982, 87-94.

point about them is that Charlemagne upgraded the silver content of his deniers without increasing the face-value. This seems to have been a bold attempt to deploy coinage as an active medium for exchange by giving it greater credibility. Charlemagne's reforms were closely followed by Offa of Mercia, and then by Pope Leo III. Grierson, in an important review of these reforms, has written

[They] involved the distribution of new standards to which it was ordered that local ones should conform. Most of these probably left existing measures much as they had been – their aim was to standardise, not to alter – but some involved fundamental modifications in the way in which measures were reckoned and drastic changes in their dimensions ... The increase in the weight of the denier by a third implies a comparable change in the weight of the lb ... The light Carolingian denier (of pre-794) still conformed to the barleycorn system, for like the Merovingian denier and the Merovingian 'tremissis' it weighed 1.3g. The heavy denier of Charlemagne, however, can scarcely have belonged to the same system, for 1.7g is between 26 and 27 grains, not a very likely weight for a coin. The obvious alternative is that it was conceived of in terms of wheat grains, the most widely used alternative to the barleycorn as a basis for the weight systems of western Europe ... the simplest explanation of the introduction of the heavy Carolingian penny is in fact that it marks the transition, effected by Charlemagne, from a weight system based on the barley grain, to one based on the wheat grain.

But where did the considerable new supplies of silver come from? Grierson tentatively speculates that some of it might have come from new mines and draws attention to the rare legend *Ex me(t)allo novo* on some of these deniers. But there is no firm evidence to support the belief, and the paucity of coins with this legend favours instead the point once made by Sture Bolin that these reforms (including certain of the legends) were influenced by contemporary Abbasid coinage. Dirhems of this date certainly bear this legend in Arabic. Is there not a case for looking elsewhere for the new supplies of silver that were obtained by the Carolingian court and thereafter deployed to their advantage[8]?

Baltic trade

The answer to these questions seems to lie at the end of the Frisian trade route. The Frisian farmer-merchants, it seems, set out northwards through the maze of islands that sheltered them from the North Sea, through channels that are now reclaimed land. From Dorestad it was a day's voyage to the small settlement found recently at Medemblik. Next they could continue along the coast, protected from the North Sea by the barrier of Frisian Islands; thus they might have reached Emden, where excavations in the 1950s found a small settlement of this period. Beyond Emden lay Hamburg – a long haul. Excavations at Hamburg just after the last war located the tiny Hammaburg, the fortified enclosure protecting Carolingia's most northerly bishop, outside which the traders are known to have camped. Beyond Hamburg lay pagan countries and a choice of routes. If the sailors had followed the Jutish coastline they would have come to the emporium at Ribe, just south of Esbjerg.[9] In fact it is more likely that the traders took the shallow passage along the river Treene, and then crossed to the river Schlei. The goal for this short but arduous crossing was the great emporium of Haithabu (Hedeby), located on an inlet set back from the wide mouth of the Schlei (Fig. 43). Just as Dorestad may be an expression of the Carolingian economy in the Rhineland, so Haithabu reflects the economic development of the western Baltic, a few kilometres away.

The remains of Haithabu lie in one of the richest archaeological zones in all of Europe. Any boat leaving its harbour could quickly be voyaging across a sea as large as the Mediterranean. The importance of Haithabu therefore cannot

[8] Philip Grierson, 'Money and coinage under Charlemagne', in *Karl der Grosse* 1, Dusseldorf 1965: 501-36; Sture Bolin, 'Mohammed, Charlemagne and Ruric', *Scandinavian History Review* 1, 1953, 5-39.

[9] Richard Hodges, op. cit. in note 7, 77-81 reviews the archaeology of Medemblik, Emden, Hamburg and Ribe. See also Morgens Bencard (ed.), *Ribe Excavations 1970-76*, vol. i, Esbjerg 1981.

Fig. 43 An aerial view of Haithabu. (Courtesy Landesmuseum für Vor- und Fruhgeschichte, Schleswig)

be underestimated, and it was not ignored by Pirenne or his opponents in the debate over Europe's economic origins. However, its familiar history has been misunderstood so often than it is worth sketching it again.

Excavations just to the south of the Viking settlement have located a small eighth-century site which may have been the forerunner of the great emporium enclosed by a later tenth-century rampart. In the late eighth century Charlemagne made a treaty with the Danes. But in 808, according to the politically   partisan   Frankish   Annals,   King   Godfred commanding a confederacy of Danish chiefs broke the treaty in a rather curious way. Apparently he initiated raids on the coast around Hamburg and simultaneously launched an attack on the emporium of Reric in the neighbouring territory of the Obrodites. The Obrodites were also allies of the Carolingians, and Reric – probably the site of Alt-Lübeck – gave the Carolingians limited access to the Baltic Sea. After Godfred had sacked Reric he took the traders he discovered there to a new site he had founded at *Sliesthorp* – a corruption of Schleswig – in other words, the site we know as Haithabu (Fig. 44).

Extensive excavations have uncovered the first planned phase of Haithabu, and the timbers employed in its first dwellings and along its roads have been dated by dendrochronology to about 810/14. It appears, therefore, that the Danish king literally built a settlement (large by Scandinavian standards) close to his southern frontier and placed the supposedly captured merchants in it. The Frankish Annals also tell us that Charlemagne was particularly angry and soon marched northwards to the river Weser. He took with him an elephant that had been a gift from the Abbasid caliph, Harun al-Rashid, but it died at Luppenheim on Luneburg Heath before the enemy was engaged (see p. 121). Meanwhile, as Godfred was refurbishing the Danevirke walls – his southern defences – in the environs of Haithabu, he was assassinated by his confederates. After this the Danish chiefs sued for peace and new terms were quickly settled between the

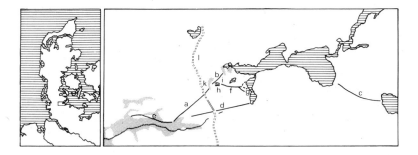

Fig. 44 The location of the Danevirke in southern Jutland, and of Haithabu (g) at its eastern terminus. (After H. Andersen)

Carolingians and the Danes. As a result, to judge from the archaeological evidence, Haithabu flourished, while Reric, if it was at Alt-Lübeck, did not.

Why did Godfred attack a neighbouring trading station, remove its merchants and then build a large, new trading station close to the border he shared with the very people he had just insulted? First, we must emphasise that the Frankish Annals probably give us a partisan view. Then we must recognise the importance and wealth of Haithabu after *c.*810 and contrast it with the tiny settlement to the south that preceded it, or with the modest trading site at Ribe to the north. On balance it looks as though Godfred was taking a great gamble, and though he did not live to see its fruits his achievement was clear enough. In fact he had persuaded the Carolingians to direct their long-distance trading operations through his territory: Haithabu now became Carolingia's access point to the Baltic.[10]

Godfred had created a place where Slavic, Swedish, Frisian and Danish traders could assemble and undertake the exchange of goods from the Carolingian Empire for Baltic Sea commodities. In addition the emporium provided the context for developing craft production for local communities. The excavators at Haithabu have brought to light the evidence of amber-, bone- and metal-working, including a wide range of jewellery. Coins were also minted here during Carolingian time (Fig. 45), closely copying Dorestad types issued during the reigns of Charlemagne and Louis. The settlement also must have contained boat-builders, shipwrights, house-builders and various smiths and carpenters. The implications of these manifold activities concentrated at one place have been pointed out by Klavs Randsborg, who has shown that the surrounding villages provided Haithabu with jointed meat. In other words, Haithabu's development had a direct impact on its region, and we can scarcely deny the brilliance of Godfred's perspicacity.

[10] Herbert Jankuhn, *Haithabu. Ein Handelsplatz der Wikingerzeit*, Neumünster 1976; see also Klavs Randsborg, *The Viking Age in Denmark*, London 1980, 85-92, 171-2 and Kurt Schietzel, Stand der siedlungsarchäologischen Forschung in Haithabu – Ergebnisse und Probleme', *Berichte über die Ausgrabungen in Haithabu* 16, 1981.

Fig. 45 An imitation of an earlier eighth-century Frisian 'wodan monster' sceatta minted at Haithabu in the early ninth century. (Courtesy Kirsten Bendixen)

How did Godfred anticipate the significance of Haithabu? The answer brings us back to the rationale for Dorestad. Godfred must have become aware of the real significance of Baltic trade to the Carolingian court. This was recognised by Sture Bolin in his critique of *Mohammed and Charlemagne* soon after it was published. In short the answer lies in the flowering of Baltic Sea commerce at the beginning of the Viking Age.

Charlemagne's earlier treaty with the Danes must reflect his awareness of a great change in the Baltic Sea economy. Archaeologists identified this development a century ago. Hjalmar Stolpe first revealed the staggering range and wealth of imported objects in the gravefields at Birka, in central Sweden. Many graves contained Islamic coins (Fig.46) and silks (Fig. 47) made in various parts of the East. Carolingian pots and glasses were also found, as well as a variety of Slavic vessels. In all, the excavations of the gravefield at Birka demonstrate the existence of complex trade patterns which began around 790 and flourished in the ninth century and again in the tenth century. These patterns link the Baltic Sea communities directly to the Caliphate, and as a result the Scandinav-

Fig. 46 Silver dirhems found at Paviken on Gotland (Courtesy Statens Historiska Museum, Stockholm)

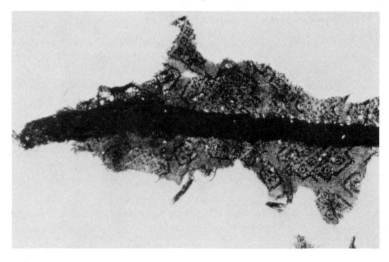

Fig. 47 A fragment of Chinese silk from a ninth-century grave at Birka, central Sweden. (Courtesy Statens Historiska Museum, Stockholm)

ians were recipients of an astonishing array of exotica and silver which cannot have failed to impress any west European merchant. Archaeologists have since uncovered other trading settlements of this type on all sides of the Baltic Sea.

Norwegian archaeologists have excavated the small emporium at Kaupang, south-west of Oslo, where the rich blend of Oriental, Baltic and Carolingian finds in its cemetery and occupation areas is as impressive as at Birka. At Löddeköpinge, close to Lund, a large trading site is currently under investigation, and it may reflect the beginnings of regional markets in Scania generated by this newborn trade. On the Swedish island of Gotland, archaeologists have long known of the large walled site of Västergarn, and in recent years a trading site was found close by at Paviken. Paviken, it now seems, may be just one of several emporia operated by the adventurous Gotlanders who possibly controlled commerce in the central Baltic area. On the south side of the Baltic Sea, to the east of Alt-Lübeck, similar sites have been found at Wollin in East Germany and at Grobin in Poland. Finally, at the eastern exit to the Baltic lies Staraja Ladoga, an emporium controlling the entrance to the river Volga and the long route via Bulgar to the Caspian Sea. Excavations at Staraja Ladoga before the First World War revealed cemeteries with plentiful evidence of Scandinavians here as early as about 800, long

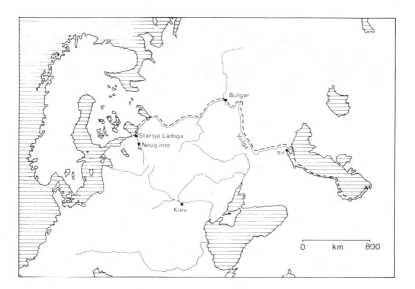

Fig. 48 The Viking route to the Orient down the Volga via Staraja Ladoga

before colonies were founded at Novgorod or Kiev controlling the Dneiper route to the Black Sea (Fig. 48).[11]

The Scandinavian traders evidently ventured south-eastwards to exchange furs, slaves and possibly metals with Moslem traders at 'Mohammadiyah' on the Caspian Sea. They then returned with Islamic silver dirhems. We know this from the many hoards in Russia and Scandinavia as well as from the few coins lost in the Baltic Sea emporia. Of course they also brought back silks, exotic metal objects like the Kashmiri buddha from Helgö (Fig. 49) and doubtless oriental spices and other foodstuffs as well. But it is the silver coins that attracted Bolin's attention when he reviewed the Pirenne thesis; these, he believed, provided the all-important silver that underpinned the Carolingian Renaissance.[12]

We have shown that the Carolingians had a strong interest in the Baltic Sea, and we have stressed the need for new supplies of silver to finance Charlemagne's coin reforms. The planned enlargement of Haithabu also fits this picture. It all adds up to a special relationship in which the Carolingians themselves remained one step removed from what was generally considered an unclean business. The dirhems were usually melted down or treated as ornaments by the Viking communities. They had no use for coins as such since they had primitive indices of value based on blood-prices and equally primitive exchange systems. Apart from the few imitations of Carolingian coins at Haithabu from about 810 to 825, there were no other Viking coins till the end of the tenth century.[13] The

[11] The trading sites in Norway and Sweden are briefly described in Hodges, op. cit. in note 7: 81-6. See Detlev Ellmers, *Frühmittelalterliche Handelsschiffart in Mittel-und Nordeuropa*, Neumünster 1972.

[12] The precise date of these Islamic coins has been the substance of a lively debate: U.S. Linder Welin, 'The first arrival of Oriental coins in Scandinavia and the inception of the Viking Age in Sweden', *Fornvännen* 69, 1974, 22-9; Johann Callmer, 'Oriental coins and the beginning of the Viking period', *Fornvännen* 71, 1976, 175-85; 1980, 203-11; D.M. Metcalf, 'Some twentieth-century runes. Statistical analysis of the Viking-Age hoards and the interpretation of wastage rates', in M.A.S. Blackburn & D.M. Metcalf (eds), *Viking-Age Coinage in the Northern Lands*, Oxford (B.A.R. International Series 122), 1981, 329-82.

[13] See Kirsten Bendixen, 'Sceattas and other coin finds', in Morgens Bencard (ed.), *Ribe Excavations 1970-76*, vol. i, Esbjerg 1981, 63-85; Birgitta

Fig. 49 The Kashmiri Buddha from Helgö, central Sweden. (Courtesy Statens Historiska Museum, Stockholm)

silver dirhems would have been readily exchanged for Rhenish wine, Rhenish jugs with tin-foil decorations (Tating ware), Rhenish glasses, Rhenish quernstones and possibly Rhenish weapons. The task of obtaining the silver, however, as well as other merchandise from the Nordic pagans was outside the

Hardh, 'Trade and money in Scandinavia in the Viking Age', *Papers of the Lund Institute* 2, 1975-77, 223-50; Metcalf, op. cit. in note 11.

range of behaviour condoned by the Carolingian Church. Consequently, it is not surprising that the Frisians – new converts and perhaps less than committed Christians – were permitted to act as agents for the Carolingian court. Nor is it surprising that the trade in dirhems has left no trace within the Empire. The Carolingian Church was zealously opposed to Islam, and the coins with their bold Arabic legends were not going to have any face value within Charlemagne's Europe. On the other hand, the form of the coins may have influenced the new Carolingian deniers, and the curious gold imitations of Islamic coins minted by King Offa of Mercia late in his life may be a rare reflection of this new source of wealth.[14]

Charlemagne did, however, contact the Abbasid caliph in Baghdad. Three Carolingian embassies were sent to the caliph's court, and at least two Abbasid missions visited Charlemagne. The history of these relations is complex. It dates back to the overthrow of the Umayyad caliph at the battle of the Zab in 750, when several of the Umayyad ruling dynasty sought refuge in Spain. There they became integrated with the ruling house in Cordoba, and by the end of the century a descendant of these refugees had risen to be the amir of Moslem Spain. Spurred on by the new Abbasid dynasty in the Middle East, a small Abbasid splinter group in Spain aimed to eliminate the Umayyad survivors. The Spanish Abbasids sought support for their cause in Pepin's Francia; he was content to oblige because the Cordoban dynasty posed a constant military threat to south-west France. Charlemagne continued his father's allegiance to the Abbasid cause in Spain, and even led an ill-fated expedition as far as Barcelona in a bid to oust the Umayyads. In recognition of this unexpected source of help, Harun al-Rashid the Abbasid caliph in Baghdad expressed interest in diplomatic relations with the Carolingians.

Pepin had sent a mission to Baghdad in 765. Charlemagne's

[14] Holger Arbman, *Schweden und das karolingische Reich*, Stockholm 1937, provides a fine review of the Carolingian material from Sweden in this period. For the gold coins: Ian Stewart, 'Anglo-Saxon gold coins', in R.A.G. Carson & C.M. Kraay (eds), *Scripta nummaria romana: essays presented to Humphrey Sunderland*, London 1978, 142-72.

first mission, however, was not until 797. In that year he sent two Franks, Sigismund and Lantfrid, with a Jew called Isaac as an interpreter. Their journey lasted three years and only Isaac returned. He was closely followed by an embassy from Baghdad, which included the governor of Egypt, Ibrahim Ibn al-Aghlab and a Persian. Together they brought a great range of riches and the famous white elephant called Abu'l-Abbas. The elephant had been owned originally by an Indian raja, and then by the caliph Al-Mahdi, before it was sent on its journey to the West. Abu'l-Abbas died on the campaign against Godfred in 810, as we noted earlier in this chapter. A second Carolingian embassy set out in 802 and returned in 806. Charlemagne's third mission left in 807 but arrived in Baghdad to find that Harun al-Rashid had just died. The eventual reply to this mission came in 813 and was cordial but not significant in either economic or political terms.[15]

We must not overestimate the importance of these missions. Neither leader could afford strong alliances with the infidel. Instead the succession of missions reflects an exchange of courtesies which were politically significant in so far as they showed that the Abbasids were anxious to treat with the West as well as Byzantium. The brief accounts of the missions lead us to believe that they were remarkable events for their time but not important to the running of either Empire.[16] Instead Charlemagne exploited (but did not initiate) a safer, indirect form of contact with Islam by way of the Dneiper, the Baltic and the North Sea. In conjunction with trade to Anglo-Saxon England and a little commerce in the Mediterranean, this northerly route offered the means for economic expansion.

In Chapter 7 we shall present the final argument in support of Bolin's thesis, illustrating that in one sense 'without Mohammed Charlemagne *would* have been inconceivable'. First, however, we must look more closely at the Islamic context for such links with the Baltic Sea traders. In so doing we have to shrug off the cultural barriers which seem to act as a greater constraint now than they evidently did eleven

[15] The history of these embassies is reviewed in F.W. Buckler, *Harunu'l-Rashid and Charles the Great*, Cambridge, Mass. 1931.

[16] Ibid., 47.

centuries ago. Archaeology clearly attests the adventurous spirit of the Frisians and Vikings, and, as we have seen, countless sites stress the scale of such interactions in the face of language difficulties. The sagas describing the Viking traders of the following centuries leave us in little doubt about their character. As Sigvat Thoadarson's eleventh-century poem 'Verses on a Journey to the East' ('*Austrfararvisur*') concludes:

> Light my mind was, lord, and
> mirthful, when on firth ways
> with glorious king the stormy
> gales did shake our sailships:
> o'er sounds of Lister bounded
> at will, with the wind bellying
> the wings of heeling keel birds.[17]

---

[17] Quoted by P.H. Sawyer, *The Age of the Vikings*, London 1971, 39.

6.   The Abbasid Caliphate

In 921-2, the Abbasid caliph al-Muqtadir dispatched a diplomatic mission to the khaganate of Bulgar on the Volga, north-east of Kuibyshev. The mission came across a trading-post of the Rus, and one of the members, Ibn Fadlan, left a vivid record of the encounter:

> Never had I seen people of more perfect physique. They are all tall as date-palms, and reddish in colour. They wear neither coat nor kaftan, but each man carries a cape which covers one half of his body, leaving one hand free. No one is ever parted from his axe, sword, and knife ...
> They are the filthiest of God's creatures ... lousy as donkeys. They arrive from their distant lands and lay their ships alongside the banks of the Volga, which is a great river, and there they build big houses on its shore ...
> On beaching their vessels, each man goes ashore carrying bread, meat, onions, milk, and *nabid* [beer?] and these he takes to a large wooden post with a face like that of a human being, surrounded by smaller figures, and behind them there are high poles in the ground. Each man prostrates himself before the large post and recites: 'O Lord, I have come from distant parts with so many girls, so many sable furs (and whatever other commodities are in his catalogue). I now bring you this offering.' He then presents his gift, and continues 'Please send me a merchant who has many dinars and dirhems and who will trade favourably with me without contradicting me ...'[1]

These were by no means the only or the first Europeans to trade with the Abbasid caliphate. As we saw in the last chapter, coin hoards from Russia and Scandinavia contain

[1] A frequently quoted passage. See, for example, J. Bronsted, *The Vikings*, Harmondsworth 1960, 247-48.

Fig. 50 Gold dinar of Abd al-Malik struck in A.D. 697-8, mounted as a pendant. Found at Siraf. (Photo: Giles Sholl)

thousands of silver coins from the mints of western and central Asia, exported in payment for furs and slaves. An analysis of 77 ninth-century hoards from European Russia reveals several periods in which dirhems were travelling northwards. In brief, Period 1 covers the first two decades of the ninth century up to the 820s, when new coins were regularly occurring in some numbers in the hoards. During Period 2, from the mid-820s until the 840s or 850s, virtually no newly minted coins were concealed in hoards; apparently only pre-820 dirhems were in circulation. Period 3 covers the next forty years, up to the 890s. During this time a small number of newly minted coins were hidden with a larger number of late eighth- and early ninth-century dirhems. Then in the 890s a new flood of freshly minted dirhems entered Russia, and the tenth- and eleventh-century hoards contain mostly coins of the period *c*.890-950. This evidence from European Russia is consistent with the two striking periods of Islamic coins found at places like Birka, in Sweden, as well as in Denmark. The message is clear: trade was passing up the river Volga from the Abbasid caliphate through the lands of the Khazars to Staraja Ladoga on the eastern Baltic seaboard. It seems to have begun in the late eighth century when the caliphs made trade treaties with the warlike Khazars who controlled the Transcaucasian routeways.[2] Yet why did this trade route through the Caucasus and up the Volga flourish in the late eighth and early ninth centuries, and then dwindle, to be eventually resumed on a massive scale at the beginning of the tenth century?

The answer lies partly in Europe with the economic reforms of Charlemagne and partly in western Asia.

The first Islamic dynasty, that of the Umayyads, was overthrown in 750. Throughout their empire, which extended from Spain to Pakistan, Arabs formed a ruling elite and the caliph depended on the army to maintain his grip. Social injustice encouraged revolt and the Umayyads were destroyed by a movement which claimed to be the liberator of the oppressed inhabitants of the eastern provinces. The movement emerged as a major threat when its leader, Mohammed b. Ali, laid claim to the caliphate on the grounds that, unlike the Umayyads, he was a member of the family of the Prophet, through his great-grandfather al-Abbas. In 747 his followers seized Merv, the capital of Khorasan. They rapidly gained control of the province and advanced westwards, taking the cities of Rayy (near Tehran) and Nihavand. Mohammed's

[2] Thomas Noonan, 'Ninth-century dirhem hoards from European Russia: a preliminary analysis', in M.A.S. Blackburn & D.M. Metcalf (eds), *Viking-Age Coinage in the Northern Lands*, Oxford (B.A.R. International Series 122) 1981, 47-118.

forces then fell upon Iraq. While one group defeated an Umayyad army near Kufa, another marched north and defeated the main Umayyad forces on the Greater Zab. In a short time, they had advanced into Syria, executed most members of the Umayyad family and established their own dynasty, which took its name from their ancestor, al-Abbas.[3]

The Umayyads had ruled from Damascus. The Abbasids sought a new capital outside Syria, which was full of supporters of the former regime (and in any case dangerously close to the Byzantine frontier), and nearer their power base in the east. Iraq was the obvious choice and the Abbasid caliphs experimented with one site after another. Abu'l Abbas (750-4) first chose Qasr ibn Hubayra, between Baghdad and Kufa, but in 752 he transferred the court to Anbar on the Euphrates. His successor, al-Mansur (754-75), built a third capital, Hashimiyah, between Kufa and Hira, but this too was abandoned.[4]

Baghdad

Al-Mansur travelled the length of the Tigris looking for the ideal site. Eventually he chose Baghdad on the west bank, at a point not far from the old Sasanian capital, where the Tigris and Euphrates are less than 40 kilometres apart and were connected by canals. The great geographer al-Muqaddasi (writing in about 985) tells how the local inhabitants assured the caliph that, by choosing Baghdad,

> Thou shalt always be surrounded by palm trees and be near water, so that if one district suffers from drought, or fails to yield its harvest in due season, there will be relief from another; while being on the banks of the as-Sarat [canal], provisions will reach thee in the boats which ply on the Euphrates. The caravans from Egypt and Syria will come by way of the desert, and all kinds of goods will reach thee from China on the sea, and from the country of the

[3] M.A. Shaban, *Islamic History: a new interpretation*, Cambridge 1976, vol. 2.
[4] K.A.C. Creswell, *Early Muslim Architecture* (second edition), London 1968, vol. 2, 1-5.

Greeks [i.e. the Byzantine empire] and from Mosul by the Tigris. Thus surrounded by rivers, the enemy cannot approach thee except in a ship or over a bridge, by way of the Tigris or the Euphrates.

With the assistance of hindsight, medieval writers were unanimous in praising the choice from the commercial point of view. Ya'qubi, writing in 842, states that the caliph chose the site because

> it is an island between the Tigris and the Euphrates. The Tigris to the east and the Euphrates to the west are the waterfronts of the world. Everything that comes on the Tigris from Wasit, Basra, Ubullah, Ahwaz, Fars [presumably Siraf: see p. 133], Oman, *Yamamah* [southern Arabia], Bahrain and their vicinity can go up [to Baghdad] and anchor there. In the same way, whatever is carried by boat (down) the Tigris from Mosul, Rabi'ah, Azarbaijan and Armenia, and whatever is carried on boats on the Euphrates from Mudar, Raqqa, Syria, the frontier, Egypt and North Africa, can come and unload at this terminus. It can also be a meeting place for people from Jibal (the central Zagros), Isfahan, Kur and Khorasan.

Tabari (d.923) makes the caliph exclaim: 'This is the Tigris; here is no distance between us and China. Everything on the sea can come to us ...'[5]

Once the site had been chosen, the construction of the new capital proceeded at breakneck speed. The caliph himself is said to have laid the first brick in 762. A year later he transferred the court, the treasury and the army from Hashimiyah. Most medieval writers maintain that the walls were completed in 766-7. The work had occupied a huge labour force and craftsmen drawn from the Iraqi cities of Mosul, Kufa, Wasit and Basra, not to mention Syria, the Hejaz and Iran.[6]

[5] G. Hourani, *Arab Seafaring*, Beirut (Khayats Oriental Reprints 4) 1964: 64.

[6] Creswell, op. cit., vol. 2, 6-7.

Abbasid Baghdad is buried beneath the modern city for, as Guy LeStrange remarked, so wise was the choice of site that it has served as the capital of Mesopotamia almost without interruption.[7] Our knowledge of the city of al-Mansur, therefore, comes from written sources, notably Ya'qubi and al-Khatib (1002-1071), who repeated information derived from the work of al-Khwarizmi, who actually lived at Baghdad in the early ninth century. Three scholars in particular have collated the descriptions of Ya'qubi, al-Khatib and others: LeStrange, Ernst Herzfeld and Sir Archibald Creswell.[8]

The nucleus of Abbasid Baghdad was the 'round city', a circular enclosure protected by a double wall, containing the palace, the principal mosque, ministries, barracks and residential quarters. According to al-Khatib (who gives no fewer than five different estimates of the size of the city!), the architect, Rabah, recorded its diameter as 5093 cubits, or 2640 metres. If the first figure is correct, the area was 547 hectares; Ya'qubi's figure gives an area of 860 hectares.

A minute analysis of the descriptions of the round city allowed Herzfeld to offer a detailed reconstruction of the plan. Creswell, reviewing the same data, came to much the same conclusions, which can be summarised as follows:

The defences consisted of an inner wall 35 cubits (18.1 metres) high, with towers 40 cubits (20.8 metres) high at regular intervals. Beyond this was an open space and a lower outer wall, apparently without towers. The outer wall was surrounded by a water-filled moat.

Inside the defences was a concentric residential zone, divided into quadrants by vaulted passages leading from the main gates to a central walled enclosure, containing the palace, the mosque and the government offices. The palace of al-Mansur, known as the Palace of the Golden Gate, stood in the middle of the enclosure. It was a square building, 400 cubits (208 metres) across. At the centre was a two-storey structure surmounted by a dome; the total height was 80 cubits (41.6 metres).[9]

---

[7] G. Le Strange, *Baghdad under the Abbasid Caliphate*, Oxford 1924, 12-13.
[8] Clearly summarised in Creswell, op. cit., 7-17.
[9] Ibid., 30-1.

The round city (in effect, a huge palace precinct) was by no means the only component of Abbasid Baghdad. To the south lay al-Karkh, a township which already existed in 762, while to the north was al-Harbiya, a quarter dominated by the officers of the caliph's army. Across the river stood Rusafah (laid out in 769), ash-Shammasiyah and al-Mukharrim.[10]

Baghdad was exceptionally well placed for communications by river; it was also the centre of a network of roads. Most famous of these was the 'Khorasan road' which led eastwards across the Iranian plateau from Kermanshah to Hamadan, Rayy and Nishapur, before continuing to Merv, Bukhara and Samarkand. Here the road forked, one branch striking north to Tashkent and the other leading eastwards to China.[11] This, incidentally, is the route by which silver for the Abbasid treasury arrived in Baghdad. The richest mines in the caliphate lay in the east: in Panjshir in eastern Khorasan and at Ilaq in Transoxiana. The largest single source was in the Panjshir valley and the nearby mine of Jarbaya, north of Kabul. Istakhri, Ibn Hauqal and Yaqut all describe the perilous task of extracting the ore by torchlight and the tough, gambling communities that worked the mines. The silver was collected at Andarab and exported to the West in the form of bullion or coin, via Balkh and Nishapur. For a while, the mines at Ilaq, in what is now Uzbekistan, almost rivalled the Panjshir valley, and we also read of sources in Kirgiziya and Tadzhikistan. In these cases the metal was sent to Bukhara, where much of it was converted into coin. Other sources of silver existed in Iran, and al-Hamdani tells us that 20,000 dirhems per week – about 1 million per year – were struck from the silver mined at Radrad, in Yemen.[12]

[10] J. Lassner, 'The Caliph's personal domain: the city plan of Baghdad re-examined', in A. Hourani & S.M. Stern (eds), *The Islamic City*, Oxford 1970, 103-18.

[11] G. Le Strange, *Lands of the Eastern Caliphate*, Cambridge 1930. For a convenient summary of trade routes in western Asia see B. Spuler, 'Trade in the Eastern Islamic countries in the early centuries', in D.S. Richards (ed.), *Islam and the Trade of Asia*, Oxford 1970, 11-20.

[12] J.W. Allan, *Persian Metal Technology, 700-1300 A.D.*, London (Oxford Oriental Monographs 2) 1979, 13-17.

Trade in the Arabian Sea

Seen from Baghdad, the most spectacular result of the creation of new markets in Iraq was the boom in maritime trade. This has a long history in the Persian Gulf, going back to the third millennium B.C., if not earlier. The fortunes of southern Arabia had been built not only on local products (such as frankincense), but also on goods imported from the East (such as silk, gemstones and cinnamon). Long before the Hegira, well-travelled routes connected the northern, eastern and western shores of the Arabian sea, and Ubullah, at the head of the Persian Gulf, was known as *Farj al-Hind*, 'the marches of India'. For merchants from the Gulf, the main area of operations extended from Aden to Gujarat, and by the sixth century the Sasanians had established a factory in Sri Lanka. Cosmas Indicopleustes wrote of 'Persian Christians who have settled there' and described how 'from all India, Persia and Ethiopia many ships come to this island ... From the farther regions – I refer to *Tsinista* [China] and other places of export – the imports of Sri Lanka are silk, aloes, cloves, sandalwood and so forth]... [which are passed on] to Persia, *Homerite* [in Yemen] and *Adoulis* [in Ethiopia]'. Tabari, Hamza of Isfahan and Tha'alibi even believed that Khusro I (531-78/9) conquered Sri Lanka, and although the claim is preposterous it may well reflect the dominant role of Sasanians in the island's trade with the west. As Procopius complained, 'it was impossible for [Byzantium's allies] the Ethiopians to buy silk from the Indians, for Persian merchants always locate themselves at the very harbours where the Indian ships first put in ... and are accustomed to buy the entire cargoes'.[13]

Even in the first few centuries A.D. the compiler of the *Periplus of the Erythraean Sea* had information about not only Sri Lanka, but also the east coast of India, and western merchandise (including wine and table wares from the Mediterranean) reached Arikamedu (near Pondicherry) in some quantity.[14] Centuries later, we even have the hint of a

[13] D. Whitehouse & A. Williamson, 'Sasanian maritime trade', *Iran* 11 1973, 29-49. The quotation is from Procopius, *Wars* 1. 20.12.

[14] R.E.M. Wheeler with A. Ghosh & K. Deva, 'Arikamedu: an Indo-

Sasanian emporium on the Malay peninsula. It is contained in a letter of Ishoyahb III (647 or 650-657/8), catholicus of the Nestorian church, who reports that the metropolitan of *Rev Ardashir* (in the Persian Gulf) was responsible for the church in 'India', by which he meant a region extending 'from the maritime borders of the Sasanian kingdom to the country called *QLH*, which is a distance of 12000 parasangs'. Syriac *QLH* is taken to be the same as the Arabic *Qal'ah*, the name given by westerners to a port in Burma or Malaysia. The implied existence of a Nestorian church at Qal'ah indicates at least occasional contact with the West.[15]

Tabari, Baladhuri and Dinawari all wrote of 'China ships' in the port of Ubullah at the time of the Moslem conquest. Unfortunately, the phrases they use (*sufun min al-sin* and *sufun siniyah*) are open to more than one interpretation, and it is not clear whether our sources meant 'Chinese ships' or 'ships that sail to China', or even 'ships carrying Chinese merchandise'.[16] We cannot exclude the possibility, therefore, that some ships from the Far East sailed to the Gulf just as (regardless of the identity of the *Possu* who appear in the Chinese sources and are sometimes taken to be Persians) some ships from the West may have ventured beyond Sri Lanka. Nevertheless as far as regular traffic was concerned, at the time of the Hegira, Sri Lanka was the customary terminus for sailings from both the Far East and the West.

By the end of the Abbasid period, the pattern had changed and ships from Siraf (on the Iranian coast of the Gulf) and Sohar (on the Sea of Oman) made regular voyages not only to Sri Lanka, but also to China and East Africa. Both Ibn Khurdadbih and the author of *Akhbar al-Sin w'al-Hind* described the route to China. According to the latter, ships either coasted to Daibal (in the Indus delta) before striking

---

Roman trading station on the east coast of India', *Ancient India* 2, 1946, 17-124. The most recent translation of the *Periplus* is by G.W.B. Huntingford, *The Periplus of the Erythraean Sea*, London 1980.

[15] B.E. Colless, 'Persian merchants and missionaries in medieval Malaya', *Journal of the Malaysian Branch of the Royal Asiatic Society* 42, 1969, 10-47, esp. 21ff.

[16] Hourani, op. cit. in note 5, 46-50.

south, or took advantage of the monsoon and sailed directly to *Kulam* (Quilon) in south India. They then rounded Sri Lanka and made for the Nicobar Islands, where they took on food and water, and Qal'ah. The final stages of the journey took them through the Malacca Strait to ports in Vietnam and their ultimate goal, the warehouses of *Khanfu* (Canton) in southern China. The voyage from Oman took 120 days, excluding stops.[17] In Canton, foreign merchants were assigned special quarters and were required to place their goods in a bonded warehouse. At the end of the sailing season, when all the merchants had arrived, the goods were released from bond, three-tenths were taken as duty and the rest was sold to the highest bidders. The Chinese government had the right of pre-emption but, *Akhbar* reports, it paid the highest prices. Trade with the East brought to the Gulf silk, paper, porcelain and many commodities from China; drugs, spices and aromatic wood from south-east Asia; tin from Malaysia; rubies and other gemstones from Sri Lanka; and pepper from India. It brought gold, ivory, slaves and timber from East Africa. The voyages were hazardous and immensely long (the round-trip to China was 16,000 kilometres), but the profits were high. 'I have met Ali al-Hili,' someone noted in the twelfth century, 'and he told me that when he came back from China ... his merchandise was worth half a million dinars.'[18]

The first detailed account of trade with Africa is that of Mas'udi, who went there at least twice, the last occasion being in 917. While most merchants dealt with entrepôts on the coast, at least one enterprising Sirafi visited the interior. Mas'udi reported that the most distant ports of call were Sofala (near Beira in Mozambique) and *Waq Waq* (which has been identified variously as Madagascar, the Comores or part of the African mainland). The journey from Sohar to Sofala was a round-trip of nearly 12,000 kilometres: not as long as the voyage to China, but enormous none the less.[19]

[17] Ibid., 69-75.

[18] S.M. Stern, 'Ramisht of Siraf, a merchant millionaire of the twelfth century', *Journal of the Royal Asiatic Society*, 1967, 1-14.

[19] J. Spencer Trimingham, 'The Arab geographers and the East African coast', in H.N. Chittick & R.I. Rotberg (eds), *East Africa and the Orient*, New York and London 1975, 115-46.

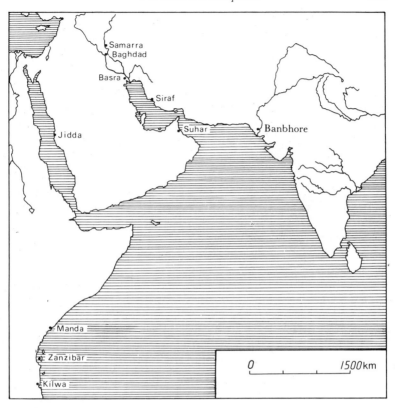

Fig. 51 Location of Siraf and other major Indian Ocean sites with which it had contacts during and after the Abbasid period

The ports

So far, we have described Abbasid maritime trade on the basis of written descriptions. In the last twenty years, however, excavations have taken place at several of the ports described by Istakhri, Mas'udi and others. As a result of its commercial activities, one port in particular became notoriously rich: Siraf, on the Persian Gulf (Fig. 51). It was not the only wealthy port on the Gulf (Basra before the Zanj rebellion was another), but in the present context it is of special significance: first; because its wealth was derived almost entirely from the network of trade which supplied Iraq with the products of Africa, India

Fig. 52 An aerial view of Siraf

and the Far East; secondly, because it has been excavated on a generous scale.[20]

The remains of Siraf stand on the Iranian coast, 200 kilometres south of Shiraz (Fig. 52). At this point, the Zagros Mountains, which form the western edge of the Iranian plateau, extend almost to the shore, leaving a coastal strip less than one kilometre wide. The medieval city developed round a shallow bay, sandwiched between the mountains and the sea. The bay affords a sheltered anchorage, and one of the few caravan routes between the Gulf and interior ran from Siraf to Shiraz, the regional capital (Fig. 53). Otherwise the environment has little to offer; the landscape is rugged and the climate severe, with high temperatures and low rainfall.

Until the excavations began in 1966, we knew nothing about Siraf before the ninth century. The excavations revealed that it was already a port in the Sasanian period, with a fort and other buildings immediately above the beach and a

[20] D. Whitehouse, 'Siraf: a medieval port on the Persian coast', *World Archaeology* 2, 1970, 141-58; 'Siraf: a medieval city on the Persian Gulf'. *Storia della Città* 1, 1976, 40-55.

Fig. 53 Siraf today: fishing boats drawn up on the beach. (Photo: David Whitehouse)

citadel on high ground overlooking the bay. In the hills behind
the site are numerous rock-cut tombs, apparently the
ossuaries of a Zoroastrian community. Among the finds from
the buildings on the shore are sherds of Red Polished ware,
imported from north-west India in the first few centuries A.D. –
clear proof of long-distance trade. Other finds include a
Roman coin of the fourth century and a gold *solidus* of the
Byzantine emperor Constans II, minted in 651-9.   coin

Although we know now that Siraf was already a port in the
Sasanian period, we also know that it became exceptionally
wealthy only in the late eighth or early ninth century. The
evidence comes partly from ninth- to eleventh-century
documents and partly – but much more convincingly – from
the excavations of 1966-73. Both sources give an exciting
impression of prosperity and long-distance communications in
the period *c*.800-1050.

Most of the written evidence consists of travellers' memoirs,
which describe the wealth of Siraf and the fortunes to be made
from trade with China and other distant countries. The fullest
account was compiled by Istakhri, writing in about 950, who
states that the city was almost as large as Shiraz, the capital
of Fars. Despite the poverty of the environment, the

community flourished and merchants spent huge sums on
building fine multistorey houses. The goods which enriched
the bazaar included ambergris, gemstones, ivory, spices and
pearls. Siraf prospered, we are told, until the late tenth
century, when a decline set in. Muqaddasi maintained that an
earthquake in 977 frightened away many of the merchants. By
1100, Kish, an island port 100 kilometres down the coast, had
usurped the former supremacy of Siraf.

This, in a nutshell, is the documentary evidence; survey and
excavation tell the same story, but in greater – and tangible –
detail. The medieval city extended along the shore for four
kilometres (Fig. 54). Curtain walls with forts and look-out
posts protected the approaches along the coastal plain. The
precipitous north face of the escarpment behind Siraf made
defences on the landward side unnecessary. As far as we
know, the waterfront was unprotected until the tenth century
– a vivid testimony to the control exercised by the Abbasids in
the Gulf. The total area of Siraf within the walls was about
250 hectares: less than half the area of the round city of
Baghdad, but very large indeed in the context of an area with
little rainfall and no perennial river. In the western part of the
city, at least 110 hectares were densely built up, with narrow
streets and few, if any, open spaces. Near the shore stood the
Friday Mosque, the bazaar and a residential quarter, with an
industrial suburb near the city wall. On higher ground, well
placed to derive maximum benefit from any breeze that blew,
were the palaces of the richest merchants. Behind these, on
the flanks of the escarpment, were the cemeteries. In the
eastern part of Siraf, permanent buildings were rare and the
area may well have contained the palm-frond huts of a large
working population.

In a traditional Islamic city, the most important public
building is the mosque. The principal mosque at Siraf stood in
the bazaar. The earliest structure, built at the beginning of the
'ninth century, was a rectangular building with a central
courtyard and a covered sanctuary facing Mecca (Fig. 55). The
mosque was rebuilt on a larger scale, also in the ninth century,
and subsequently underwent modification and repair until its
abandonment in the twelfth or thirteenth century.

The bazaars extended along the waterfront for at least a

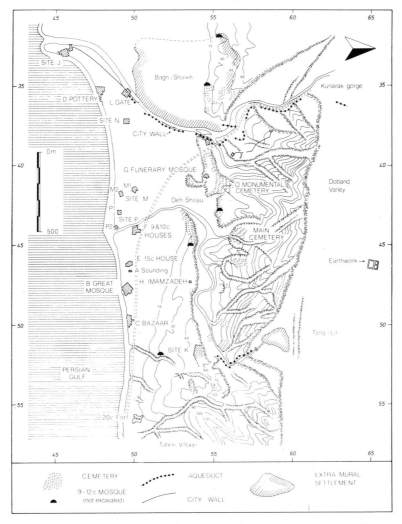

Fig. 54 A plan of the medieval city of Siraf showing the areas excavated in 1966-73.

kilometre. An area excavation near the Friday Mosque revealed that the most common features were rows of one-room shops on either side of narrow streets, which may have been covered. At one point, the excavation disclosed a sequence of occupation spanning more than two centuries, throughout which (to judge by working debris found in all

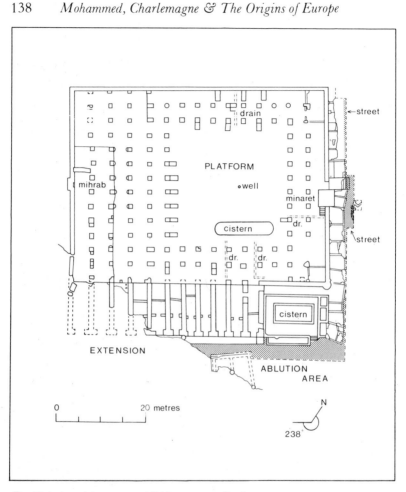

Fig. 55 A plan of the excavated Friday mosque, Siraf

periods) the area was occupied by coppersmiths – an indication that different crafts were concentrated in different parts of the bazaar (Fig. 56). Nearby were a small mosque and a public bath.

The excavation of part of a prosperous residential quarter indicated the nature of public planning and private wealth at Siraf (Fig. 57). The quarter had a gridded plan, with a main street and narrow alleys at regular intervals, dividing one house from the next. The houses contained the same basic elements.

Fig. 56 The bazaar (site C) at Siraf with remains of a mosque (left), and a *hammam* (bath-house) to the right. (Photo: Joseph Cloutman)

Fig. 57 Part of the residential quarter (site F), Siraf. (Photo: Giles Sholl)

Fig. 58 The courtyard of a tenth-century house at Siraf. (Photo: Giles Sholl)

The entrance passage gave access to a paved courtyard (Fig. 58). On the ground floor, most of the rooms were entered from the yard, suggesting that this was the focal point of communal activity. The walls of two of the houses survived to heights of more than four metres, showing that the buildings were at least two storeys high. Carved and moulded stucco was common.

Among the buildings on high ground above the bazaar were five large complexes, each with several courtyards and one or more private cisterns. Partial excavation of the largest complex revealed a palace – the only word for a residence that was larger than Longleat or Hatfield House – evidently the property of a wealthy merchant or official, possibly the governor himself.

Medieval writers contrasted the wealth of Siraf with the poverty of its environment, and modern visitors endorse this impression. Rugged mountains, dissected by deep, boulder-strewn canyons, dominate the hinterland; the soil is poor. The contrast demands an explanation, and after a detailed survey of the geomorphology, soils and traces of land-use within an irregular radius of 5-7 kilometres of Siraf, the excavators concluded that up to 700 hectares could have been cultivated.[21] These would have gone a long way towards feeding the city, but not far enough. Food was imported from the well-watered upland valleys of the interior and perhaps also from overseas – and paid for from the profits of long-distance trade.

Siraf is not the only source of archaeological information on the maritime trade of the late eighth and ninth centuries. Excavations are in progress at Sohar and have taken place at Banbhore (which is probably Daibal) in the Indus delta and at Manda and other sites on the African coast.

The site of Banbhore stands among desolate salt flats on a former mouth of the Indus, 60 kilometres from Karachi and 40 kilometres from the present-day coast.[22] As the only major site in a sparsely populated region, it is often – and plausibly – identified as Daibal. Excavations revealed that Banbhore was already occupied in the first few centuries A.D. Like Siraf and Sohar, it flourished in the ninth and tenth centuries. The Islamic town contained several well-defined elements. The walls enclosed an area just over 500 metres across. The most important building within the walls was the Congregational Mosque, which measured 41 x 43 metres and had an arcaded sanctuary facing Mecca and double arcades round the central courtyard. Among inscriptions from the mosque, none of which was found in situ, is a dedication bearing the date 109/727. Outside the walls, the excavators found an industrial quarter and a pool surrounded by a stone revetment: either a reservoir or, more probably, an enclosed harbour. The site as a whole is littered with imported pottery: Chinese stoneware, white glazed table wares from Iraq and coarse pottery from the Persian Gulf. Like Siraf, Banbhore stood on a barren coast, which could not have supported a town without the wealth generated by trade. It served as a port of call for ships voyaging between India and the Gulf, and as the outlet for

[21] T. Wilkinson, 'Agricultural decline in the Siraf region, Iran', *Paleorient* 2, 1974, 123-32.

[22] F.A. Khan, *Banbhore* (third edition), Karachi 1969. For interim and specialist reports see *Pakistan Archaeology* 1, 1964, 49-55; 3, 1966, 65-90 (on Arabic inscriptions from the site); 5, 1968, 176-85; 6, 1969, 117-209 (on the coins and the congregational mosque).

commodities from up country: lapis lazuli (from the Hindu Kush), musk (from the Himalayas), indigo and other items of trade.

On the opposite side of the Arabian Sea, we have written information about the involvement of East Africa in the ninth century, but no detailed account until a hundred years later, when Mas'udi recalled seeing ships from Siraf and Sohar as far south as Sofala. But thanks largely to the work of Neville Chittick we now possess archaeological evidence for the period of commercial expansion under the early Abbasids. In 1960-5 Chittick excavated at Kilwa in Tanzania and subsequently worked at Manda in Kenya.[23]

The ruins of Kilwa stand on a small inshore island, 250 kilometres south of Dar es-Salaam. For three hundred years before the arrival of the Portuguese, Kilwa was the wealthiest port on the East African coast. In the period which interests us, the settlement was small. Stone buildings were rare, perhaps non-existent. Fishing and gathering shellfish played an important part in the subsistence economy and the only industries recognised by the excavators were iron-working and the manufacture of shell beads. One short inscription shows that there were Moslems in the town. Imported pottery (less than one per cent of the total) and small objects point to contacts with western Asia. But there was little sign of wealth, and our overall impression is of a coastal settlement with a handful of Moslem traders dealing in commodities (perhaps ivory) from the interior.

Manda presents a different picture. Like Kilwa, Manda was on an inshore island. Traces of stone buildings cover about 10 hectares, and a further 10 hectares are strewn with potsherds, but not rubble; presumably they were occupied by gardens or huts. A masonry revetment, built to protect the settlement from marine erosion, contains blocks of coral weighing more than a tonne – a scale of construction without parallel elsewhere in Africa south of the Sahara, not even at Great Zimbabwe. The finds include an astonishing amount of

[23] H.N. Chittick, 'Discoveries in the Lamu Archipelago', *Azania* 2, 1967, 1-31; *Kilwa: an Islamic trading city on the East African coast*, Nairobi (British Institute in Eastern Africa Memoir 5) 1974.

imported pottery: 30 per cent of the sample – one pot in three – consists of glazed sherds from Iraq, Chinese white and green stonewares, even coarse ware from the Persian Gulf. Evidently we are dealing with something special, and the explanation may well be timber. Manda is an inhospitable place with only one asset: it is surrounded by mangrove swamps. Palm trunks apart, the coasts of southern Arabia and the Persian Gulf have no timber for building. Nevertheless flat roofs of matting and mud resting on poles are ubiquitous. The poles are placed at intervals of 0.2-0.3 metres with the ends resting on the tops of the walls, and even a modest building requires dozens; Siraf alone must have used millions. Until recently, East Africa provided most of the supply, exporting tens of thousands of mangrove poles a year to Arabia.[24] Manda, a rich site surrounded by mangroves, suggests that the trade began in (or before) the Abbasid period, when local supplies (mangroves once grew in the Gulf) were exhausted.

The expansion of trade

The time has come to attack the question: When, between the seventh and the tenth centuries, did merchants from the Gulf extend the range of their regular voyaging to include China and East Africa, which are separated by almost a quarter of the world's circumference?

The question has been answered on more than one occasion, on the basis of written evidence. Hourani, for example, reminded us of the Omani, Abu Ubayda al-Saghir, who visited China towards the middle of the eighth century and of a merchant from Basra who was financing trade with China in about 775. In 825, a fleet was sent from Basra to punish the pirates of Bahrain who preyed on ships from China, India and Iran. Buzurg b. Shahriyar (writing in the mid-tenth century) recalled that the first captain to visit China regularly was one Abharan, but he did not record the date. Nevertheless Hourani drew the conclusion that 'by the

[24] A.H.J. Prins, 'The Persian Gulf dhows: two variants in maritime enterprise', *Persica* 1959: H. Yajima, *The Arab Dhow Trade in the Indian Ocean: preliminary reports*, Tokyo (Studia culturae Islamicae 3) 1976.

middle of the ninth century it is certain that there was regular sailing to China'.

The archaeological evidence now at our disposal allows us to offer a more precise solution. The vital information comes from the Congregational Mosque at Siraf, where at least three, and possibly five, phases of construction have been recognised.[25] The original mosque was a rectangular building 51 metres long and 44 metres wide, standing on a platform 2 metres high. Not long after it was built, the mosque was enlarged in either one or two operations. Later it was restored, again in one or two operations. The mosque was built on the remains of a fort and other structures of the Sasanian and early Islamic periods. In the terminology used when discussing the finds, the fort and the other early buildings belong to periods B1-4; the mosque was constructed in period B5 and enlarged in B6. The mosque was surrounded by a bazaar, in which the earliest structures were associated with the same range of pottery and coins as the building and the enlargement of the mosque itself; its construction, therefore, is attributed to period B5 or B6.

Glazed pottery was in use throughout the history of the mosque and the buildings beneath it. The overwhelming majority (97.9 per cent) of the 'local' glazed wares consisted of fragments with yellow clay and blue-green glaze. A negligible proportion (0.1 per cent) had colourless glaze, and corrosion rendered the remaining 2 per cent indeterminate. The most distinctive form, present in periods B4-6, was a jar with barbotine decoration: a type familiar for more than fifty years, thanks to the publication of examples from Susa, Samarra and Baghdad. A striking feature of these jars, wherever they come from, is the similarity of one piece to the next. All are between 50 and 60 centimetres high and have a heavy ring base, ovoid or pear-shaped body, short tapering neck and a rim of triangular section (Fig. 59). Below the neck are three horizontal handles. Between each pair of handles is an area of robust barbotine ornament consisting of leaf scrolls or abstract motifs beneath an arc composed of two parallel lines divided by pellets. Stamped,

[25] D. Whitehouse, *Siraf III. The Congregational Mosque*, London, n.d. (1980).

Fig. 59 An earthenware jar with blue-green glaze made in southern Iraq. This type was traded to all the Indian Ocean ports. (Photo: Giles Sholl)

incised and gouged ornament also occurs.

Neutron activation analyses showed that sherds with blue-green glaze from Siraf and sites in Iraq were made from clays with the same, or very similar, combinations of trace elements. These differed from the trace elements in the clay used for potting at Siraf itself. It is reasonable to suppose, therefore, that the bulk of the pottery with yellow clay and blue-green glaze found at Siraf was imported, presumably from Iraq.

Beginning in period B3, the 'local' glazed earthenwares were associated with stoneware from China or south-east Asia (Fig. 60). The occurrence of all types of glazed pottery was as follows:[26]

[26] D. Whitehouse, *Siraf XI. Sasanian and Islamic Glazed pottery*, London, forthcoming.

Period	Chinese	Blue-green	Local Colourless	Corroded	Without glaze	Total
B6	230	2703	17	473	40684	44107
B5	1818	45426	27	329	230446	270846
B4	88	3046	0	51	37914	41099
B3	46	1321	6	212	42880	44465
B2	0	29	0	9	3265	3303
B1	0	15	1	6	904	926

Among the material from periods B1 and B2 were sherds of Indian Red polished ware from Gujarat. The Far Eastern finds from periods B3 and B4 consisted of fragments of 'Dusun' and black glazed jars. In periods B5 and B6, they were joined by bowls with painted decoration and with pale green or yellowish glaze, patches of which have been scraped from the interior. Period 6 preceded the importation of Chinese white ware and its Islamic imitations.

The finds may be interpreted as follows:

Periods B1 and B2. Siraf was in touch with Iraq and Gujarat.

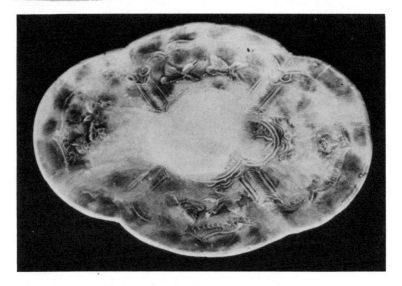

Fig. 60 A Chinese dish from Siraf. (Photo: Joseph Cloutman)

China.

Periods B3 and B4. Direct or indirect trade with China had begun, although the stoneware jars accounted for only 0.1 per cent of the pottery in period B3 and 0.2 per cent in B4.

Period B5. The mosque was built. About this time, 17.1 per cent of all the pottery was glazed: a higher percentage than at any other period in the history of Siraf. At least 16.3 per cent of the pottery had blue-green glaze and jars with barbotine ornament were common. The range and quantity of Chinese ceramics had increased; now they included table wares as well as jars and accounted for 0.7 per cent of the entire sample, or 4.1 per cent of the glazed pottery.

Period B6. The mosque was enlarged. The range of Islamic and Far Eastern glazed pottery was virtually the same as in period B5, but the quantities had declined to 7.2 per cent and 0.5 per cent respectively.

Jars with blue-green glaze and barbotine ornament have an exceptionally wide distribution in Africa and south and south-east Asia. At Manda, for example, Chittick found pottery with blue-green glaze in the earliest archaeological deposits, which preceded the arrival of Chinese and Islamic white wares.

Let us return to Siraf. The evidence for the absolute chronology of periods B3-6 was as follows:

Period B3. A long period of occupation. Latest coin (sealed by a late floor): Umayyad or early Abbasid. Suggested date: ended *c*. 750-75.

Period B4. Two coins only, both Umayyad or early Abbasid. Suggested date: between *c*. 750-75 and *c*. 815-25.

Period B5. Latest legible coins: from the platform, 188/803-4; from the steps, 199/814-15. Suggested date: *c*. 815-25.

Period B6. Latest legible coin: *c*. 188/803-4. Suggested date: not later than *c*. 850.

The implications of all this are obvious. Siraf, which as a city had no raison d'être other than as an entrepôt for ships voyaging to and from the Arabian Sea, was trading with India

long before the eighth century and was, therefore, a Sasanian
port. By the second half of the eighth century, if not before,
stoneware jars (containers for perishable merchandise) began
to arrive at Siraf, as a result either of direct contact with China
or of trading with middlemen, perhaps in Sri Lanka. We are
reminded of Abu Ubayda al-Saghir and the merchant of
Basra, both of whom were involved in the China trade in
about 750-75.

In the early ninth century, Siraf and the pattern of its
overseas trade was transformed. The construction of the
Congregational Mosque (and perhaps also the bazaar), which
required a considerable investment of wealth, coincided with a
spectacular increase in the quantity and variety of glazed
pottery used in the town. Islamic glazed wares (which not
only cost more than pottery without glaze to produce, but also
seem to have been imported) now accounted for 17.1 per cent
of all the pottery (compared with 7.5 per cent in the preceding
period). The Chinese ceramics now included table wares and
amounted to 0.7 per cent of all the pottery in use (compared
with 0.2 per cent). One cannot avoid the conclusion that
foreign trade had reached an unprecedentedly high level and
now included direct contact with China.

At about the same time, trade with Africa increased. The
distribution of jars with blue-green glaze and barbotine
decoration, which were shown at Manda to have arrived
before the first Chinese or Islamic white wares, strongly
suggests that ships from the Gulf or Oman had ventured far
south of the equator before about 850.

We arrive, therefore, at a new answer to the question: When
did merchants from the Gulf begin to trade with China and
southern Africa on a regular basis? As far as China is
concerned, the sudden rise in the quantity of Chinese ceramics
at Siraf (from 0.2 per cent to 0.7 per cent) in period B5
suggests that direct trade began before the completion of the
mosque in about 815-25. Such precision is impossible in the
case of the African trade, since jars with barbotine ornament
remained in use after about 815-25 and our only indication of
date comes from Manda, where contact with the Gulf had
begun before the importation of white wares, which may not
have come into use until about 850, or even later.

Be that as it may, one cannot escape the conclusion that the China trade was under way well before *c.* 850 (the date suggested by Hourani); indeed, it seems to have begun before *c.* 815-25. According to Chinese sources, after a raid by *Ta-shih* and *Possu* (whoever they may have been) in 758, the port of Canton was closed to foreigners until 792.[27] It seems to us that the foundation of Baghdad in 762 helped to create a rich consumer market in Iraq, the reopening of Canton thirty years later made possible direct trade with China and the finds from Siraf show convincingly that trade had begun (and generated enough wealth to build the mosque and perhaps also the bazaar) by about 815-25. The range of long-distance trade with Africa increased at the same time, or slightly later. In any case, when we read of Bahraini pirates preying on ships from China, India *and Iran* in 825, it is difficult to doubt that they were attacking ships bound for Basra from Siraf. If we were to venture a final hypothesis, it would be that the age of expansion of Abbasid maritime trade began in the caliphate of Harun al-Rashid (786-809).

Internal politics, 775-892

The Abbasids created a new focus of wealth in Iraq and stimulated an almost meteoric increase in the range and volume of seaborne trade, which now embraced not only India, but Africa and the Far East. This commercial expansion followed rapidly on the foundation of Baghdad in 762, and the evidence from Siraf shows that by the beginning of the ninth century the quantity of maritime trade had reached an unprecedentedly high level. At precisely this period Abbasid silver was pouring into Russia, Scandinavia and north-west Europe. About 820, however, the supply of coin to the north declined and remained short for the rest of the ninth century. We have no reason to suppose that the demand in Europe and Scandinavia collapsed, or that the Volga trade route was cut. The explanation, therefore, lies in Asia, where two factors immediately capture our attention: the continuing failure of the caliphate to achieve political

[27] Hourani, op. cit. in note 5, 66.

stability and the gross extravagance of individual caliphs.[28]

First, internal politics. The caliph al-Mansur died in 775. Although his successor, al-Mahdi (d. 785), adopted a conciliatory attitude towards religious and nationalist minorities (such as the Shi'ites and members of the *Zandaqa* movement in Iran, which opposed the caliphate), the third Abbasid caliph, al-Hadi, attempted to suppress them. The aggressive policy of al-Hadi simply aggravated an already difficult situation and divided the ruling family. The caliph was assassinated in 786. His successor, Harun al-Rashid, inherited a sea of troubles. Iran was on the point of revolt and eventually the rulers of the Maghreb declared their independence. The economy, however, was booming and the caliph amassed an enormous fortune.

At the death of Harun, a power struggle erupted. Al-Amin usurped the throne, and his rival, al-Mamun, laid siege to Baghdad. Al-Amin held out for more than a year, during which the city was extensively damaged. In the end he was taken and executed, and al-Mamun, a former governor of Khorasan, abandoned Baghdad and established the court at Merv. It was a short-sighted move. In 817 an anti-caliph was proclaimed in Iraq and fighting broke out between the cities of Wasit, Kufa and Baghdad. After restoring order, al-Mamun returned to the former capital in 819. He died there in 833.

The reign of the next caliph, al-Mutasim (d. 842), was also blighted by attempted coups d'état. Remembering the civil war between al-Amin and al-Mamun, al-Mutasim imported foreign slaves – Turks, Slavs and Berbers – to form a large (and extremely expensive) praetorian guard. The price was higher than he thought. Disputes broke out between the citizens of Baghdad and the caliph's guards. For this reason (Ya'qubi tells us) al-Mutasim decided to remove the court. After a brief sojourn at Raqqa, he established a new capital, Samarra.

The court remained at Samarra for nearly fifty years (836-82). It was a period of palace revolutions and widespread unrest. Two caliphs were assassinated, two others forced into exile. Baghdad was besieged again (865-6). In Egypt, the

[28] Shaban, op. cit. in note 3, vii-viii *et passim*.

Abbasid governor, Ibn Tulun, was an independent ruler in all but name. In southern Iraq, the armies of Zanj (African) slaves, who worked in the fields and sugar plantations, rebelled in 868. The slave revolt lasted fourteen years, during which Basra was sacked and Wasit theatened. At times, the trade route from the Gulf was closed. When, in 892, al-Mutadid ascended the throne, the treasury was empty.

Samarra

It was not only the cost of maintaining the army and repairing the ravages of civil war that drained the Abbasid treasury, but also the reckless extravagance of the Abbasids themselves. We are not talking about the life-style at court (although this was notorious), but building on a gigantic scale. The works of al-Mansur at Baghdad were dwarfed by those of al-Mutasim and his successors at Samarra, for in *forty-six years* they created a city which sprawled along the Tigris for *35 kilometres*: from Woolwich, as it were, to Kew (Fig. 61).[29]

Ya'qubi provides a long account of the founding and construction of Samarra. The caliph inspected a number of possible sites before visiting Samarra, 120 kilometres upstream from Baghdad. The area was desolate and the only inhabitants were the monks of a Christian monastery. But when one of the monks recounted the legend of a former city at Samarra, which would be rebuilt by 'a great, victorious and powerful king', al-Mutasim decided to build:

> ... he had architects brought and told them to choose the most suitable positions, and they selected a number of sites for the palaces. He gave each of his followers a palace to build ... Then he had plots of ground marked out for the military and civil officers and for the people, and likewise the Great Mosque. And he had the markets drawn out round the mosque with wide market rows, all the various

[29] Astonishingly, no detailed description of the site has ever been published. For a series of aerial photographs, see Ernst Herzfeld, *Ausgrabungen von Samarra VI. Geschichte der Stadt Samarra*, Berlin 1948. For clear descriptions of the principal monuments, see Creswell, op. cit. in note 4.

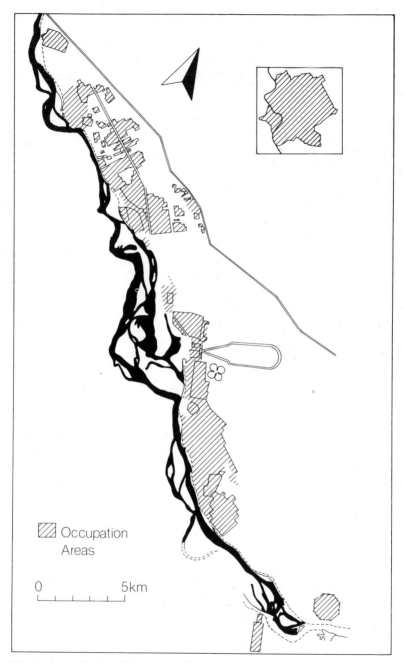

Fig. 61 A sketch plan of Samarra on the banks of the river Tigris (inset an outline
plan showing Imperial Rome for comparison)

Occupation
Areas

0   5km

kinds of merchandise being separate ... according to the arrangement after which the markets of Baghdad [and Siraf] were designed. He wrote for workman, masons and artisans, such as smiths, carpenters and all other craftsmen to be sent, and for teak and other kinds of wood, and for palm trunks to be brought from Basra ... Baghdad ... and from Antioch and other towns on the Syrian coast, and for marble workers and men experienced in marble paving to be brought.

Ya'qubi goes on to record that the Turkish troops were allocated separate quarters and to list members of the caliph's retinue who were given grants of land, on condition that they constructed bazaars, bath-houses and mosques for their followers. Main streets were laid out, canals dug and palm trees imported for planting. 'The ground had lain fallow for thousands of years, so everything that was planted or sown there flourished.' Craftsmen were imported to supply the population: papyrus makers from Egypt, potters from southern Iraq and so on. It was the caliph's clear intention to create and populate a new city, virtually overnight.

The most spectacular buildings of al-Mutasim and his successors were, in chronological order:

1. The Jausaq al-Khaqani, al-Mutasim's palace, built between 836 and 842.
2. The Great Mosque, built by al-Mutawakkil in 848/9-52.
3. The Balkuwara palace, built by al-Mutawakkil c. 849-59.
4. The Mosque of Abu Dhulaf, also built by al-Mutawakkil in 860-1.
5. The Qasr al-Ashiq, al-Mutamid's palace, built in 878-82.

The Jausaq al-Khaqani was the largest building of them all. Its walls enclosed 175 hectares, 71 of which were occupied by gardens along the Tigris (Fig. 62). A flight of steps, 60 metres wide, ascended from the gardens to a monumental entrance, the Bab al-Amma. Beyond the entrance stood the nucleus of the palace, some 200 metres square, containing reception rooms, the caliph's apartments and the harem. Behind the nucleus was a courtyard, 380 metres long; to either side were quarters for the caliph's retinue and guards, the stables and magazines. The palace was not simply huge. In the words of one of the excavators, Ernst Herzfeld:

> The magnificance ... was in keeping with this composition ... The dadoes of the walls were everywhere decorated with stucco ... [although] in the throne rooms ... [they] are replaced by similar ones of carved marble ... The upper parts of the walls of the Harim were decorated with fresco paintings ... All woodwork, doors, beams, and ceilings were of teak-wood, carved and painted, or only painted and partly gilded.[30]

The Balkuwara palace was almost as huge, consisting of a rectangular walled area of 1,250 metres a side, overlooking the Tigris. Along the river were gardens with richly decorated pavilions. The main building, which contained the throne room, royal apartments, etc., measured 465 by 255 metres. Beyond this lay an even larger compound with courtyards, mosques and other buildings. The walls of the main palace were decorated with paintings and stucco, while the principal entrance had glass mosaics.

The latest of the caliph's palaces at Samarra, the Qasr al-Ashiq, was also the smallest: a rectangular building, with imposing bastioned walls, which measured a mere 140 by 93 metres. It stood on a platform, partly natural and partly composed of vaulted substructures, with a magnificent view of the city.

The caliph al-Wathik (842-7) consolidated the foundations of Samarra laid by al-Mutasim, and Ya'qubi tells us that, thanks to his efforts, the people realised that the city was intended as a permanent capital. From this moment it attracted inhabitants. When, therefore, al-Mutawakkil constructed the Great (Congregational) Mosque, he produced a building as impressive in its proportions as the palaces. The Great Mosque measured 240 by 156 metres internally, with a sanctuary 25 bays wide and 9 bays deep. Muqaddasi reports that it rivalled the Great Mosque of Damascus and had walls

---

[30] Quoted by Creswell op. cit. vol. 2, 232-43.

Fig 62 An aerial view of the Ja'fariya palace complex (Photo courtesy Institute of Archaeology, University of London)

covered with ornament: glass mosaics with a gold ground, to judge from the tesserae found by Herzfeld when he cleared part of the interior. Outside the mosque was a free-standing minaret, more than 50 metres high.

Ya'qubi tells us that, not content with constructing the Balkuwara palace and the Great Mosque, al-Mutawakkil 'resolved to build himself a city ... so that his memory should be preserved'. In 859/60 he laid out a new quarter, Ja'fariya, containing a palace, houses, bazaars and a new congregational mosque known as the Mosque of Abu Dhulaf, which measured 213 by 135 metres internally (Fig. 62).

Each of these buildings was prodigious: the Jausaq al-Khaqani was larger than Versailles, the Great Mosque the largest ever built. While size alone is no criterion of quality, it is a measure of effort and, therefore, expenditure. And while the principal building material (sun-dried brick) and labour were cheap, the collective cost of the five buildings just described – not to mention the rest of the city – must have been immense. In the century between the reign of Harun al-Rashid (786-809) and the accession of al-Mutadid (892), the Abbasid caliphs went from fabulous wealth to bankruptcy, and lost revenues from rebellious provinces apart, an important one of the ingredients in the recipe for disaster must have been the creation of Samarra, aptly described as an 'act of folly on a vast scale'.[31]

Five conclusions

This chapter and the one before lead us to five conclusions:

1. Baghdad (founded in 762), thanks to its position and the presence of the Abbasid court, rapidly became the centre of a great commercial network, which at the end of the eighth century and in the early ninth century expanded to include the Arabian Sea and places as far removed as southern China. The reign of Harun al-Rashid (775-809) saw the wealth of

---

[31] J.M. Rogers, 'Samarra: a study in medieval town planning', in A. Hourani & S.M. Stern (eds), *The Islamic City*, Oxford 1970, 119-55, esp. 127.

Baghdad and the volume of trade reach unprecedented heights.

2. The Abbasid caliphs failed to create internal stability, *factions* and the ninth century was a period of frequent revolts and of infighting between members of the ruling family, factions at court and the army. The legitimate successor of al-Rashid climbed to the throne over the body of a usurper; of the eight succeeding caliphs, two were assassinated and two died in exile.

3. With few exceptions, the caliphs were reckless *spendthrift* spenders. The foundation of a new capital, Samarra, in 836, demanded expenditure on a colossal scale. Al-Mutasim built a palace larger than Versailles in 836-42; al-Mutawakkil replaced it with another, almost as large, in about 849-59; al-Mutamid built a third in 878-82. The city itself extended along the Tigris for 35 kilometres.

4. The product of intermittent warfare and gross *& disaster* extravagance was an economic disaster. At the death of Harun al-Rashid, the Abbasid treasury was overflowing; on the accession of al-Mutadid (892) it was empty.

5. The high point in the exportation of silver to Scandinavia, therefore, coincided with an economic boom in western Asia in the reign of Harun. The drying-up of the supply coincided with the gradual exhaustion of the Abbasid economy.

In ch 6 H tw take a careful look at coinh, building materials add doc. evidence to show that after the capitol was moved from B, a city due to its close proximity to water and roadways, to Samarra, the large scale building and reck. spending of the A.C. led to pol. unrest, confiti in n. families and factims army cart. Islamic dirhems found in Birka, Sweden and Denmark, and Mangrove wood from Manda found in Arabia shows a system of large-scale trade, but that trade was interrupted by the decline of the A.C.

Therefore affecting C and his people who had relied on trade to get the goods they needed to maintain their elitism. This shows the sensitive, interconnected nature of the trade routes even after the F. of k

7.   The End of an Era

Baghdad was not only a great centre for traders from western Russia, but also the end of a trade-route that stretched to China. Under the Abbasids it had become the centre of the world. Sture Bolin and Maurice Lombard recognised this long ago in their critiques of Pirenne's thesis, but the evidence was not sufficient to convince their fellow historians. Today, we have far more information at our disposal. What do we make of it? How should we explain the sudden and almost simultaneous development of Dorestad, Haithabu, Birka – and Siraf? Each emporium, as we have seen, was linked by a network of traders – one operating in the North Sea; one in the western and another in the eastern Baltic; and one in the Arabian Sea. So while we might concur with Bolin in likening the traders operating the Dneiper route – the last one in the chain – to the treasure fleets of the Spanish bringing silver from the New World in the sixteenth century, we should not forget that they were links in a long and complex chain.[1]

Why was the direct sea route from the east to Italy, the southern flank of the Carolingian Empire, ignored? After all, the embassies between Harun al-Rashid and Charlemagne took this route, from Pisa and Genoa to the Emperor's court. Two reasons may explain why the merchants failed to follow the ambassadors. First, the embassies between the two leaders amounted to the barest signs of concord. Spiritual revivals were occurring in both societies at this time, creating ever-deepening divisions between Christianity and Islam. The infidel was therefore forcefully condemned in both communities. The two leaders probably recognised what relations were politically acceptable to their subjects and what were not. As F.W. Buckler shows in his brief account of the embassies between Charlemagne and Harun al-Rashid,

[1] Sture Bolin, 'Mohammed, Charlemagne and Ruric', *Scandinavian Economic History Review* 1, 1952.

Fig. 63 The reverse of a silver denier minted at Dorestad by Louis the Pious (Courtesy the Dutch State Archaeological Service)

the Abbasid leaders were very conscious of the possible impact the Carolingian emissaries might make in Baghdad.[2] Secondly, both empires had turbulent relations with Byzantium. The Carolingian mission of 802, for example, had to brave Byzantine warships in the Adriatic during the long journey eastwards. At this time the Carolingians and Byzantines were disputing the control of Venice. It was one of a succession of small wars between the empires. Harun al-Rashid, by contrast, was Constantinople's most feared enemy. In 781 he led an army to the walls of the Byzantine capital, and left only after a vast payment was made to him. As caliph he sent a number of expeditions into Byzantine territory, compelling Byzantine nobles to become his vassals. But the Byzantine navy remained a formidable enemy, since it was the only means by which Constantinople could defend its farflung islands, as well as the south of Italy. This navy discouraged the two land-based powers from exploring their unlikely

[2] F.W. Buckler, *Harunu'l-Rashid and Charles the Great*, Cambridge, Mass., 1931, esp. 21-7.

relationship any further. As a result the Carolingians looked for 'markets' to the west and north, while the Abbasid merchants established contact with traders from western Russia and with merchants from further afield.

In the chiefdoms and states along this route from west to east, as in all petty kingdoms, the heads of government were in a tenuous position. The trade, of course, brought the rulers luxury goods which emphasised their status and prestige. But since long-distance trade was controlled by the elite, the entire system might be threatened if a crisis occurred in one link in the chain. Quite suddenly the whole chain might collapse.

Hence, to allay any doubts about the importance of Abbasid silver for the Carolingians, we must examine this domino theory. In Chapter 6 we outlined how the Abbasid dynasty staved off a political crisis by investing its vast wealth in a gigantic enterprise – the creation of Samarra. This was in part a gamble to overcome political divisions; it is a reflection of the social turmoil following the death of Harun al-Rashid. What, therefore, happened in western Europe during this unsettled period in the caliphate?

Weakening of the oriental link

The instability of the Abbasid caliphate and the monstrous spending of the caliphs are reflected in the coin-hoards found in European Russia. A new analysis of these hoards by Thomas Noonan shows that a marked change in their composition occurred in the 820s. After this date there are noticeably fewer newly minted coins from the caliphate and a declining percentage of North African and Spanish dirhems.[3] In addition, Klavs Randsborg has noted the diminishing numbers of silver dirhems in Scandinavian contexts during the second and third quarters of the ninth century.[4] It would appear, therefore, that the western Russian and Scandinavian communities felt the effects of the Abbasid upheavals. Yet

[3] Thomas S. Noonan, 'Ninth-century dirham hoards from European Russia: a preliminary analysis', in M.A.S. Blackburn & D.M. Metcalf (eds), *Viking-Age Coinage in the Northern Lands*, Oxford (B.A.R. Supplementary Series 122), 47-118, esp. 69-71.

[4] Klavs Randsborg, *The Viking Age in Denmark*, London 1980, 152-62.

while the infusion of oriental wealth diminished, the silver already in these territories continued to circulate and for a few years some places continued to prosper. The excavators of Haithabu, for example, have revealed a succession of closely-dated occupation phases spanning the ninth-century settlement. All the timber buildings were rebuilt or altered every generation or so. We also know that Haithabu still attracted traders from the Rhineland as late as 845 when a group of merchants were attacked by Vikings below the walls of Hamburg. Bishop Rimbert described the scene in a vivid passage, and we are left in little doubt of its significance for the traders:[5]

> The surprising swiftness of this event allowed no time for the men from the surrounding area to assemble. When the lord bishop first heard of the appearance of the enemy, he first of all wanted to defend the place using the inhabitants of the castle and of the unfortified *wik* until reinforcements arrived. However, the heathens attacked and the castle was already encircled. He now appreciated the importance of defending the outer areas and pondered how he might save the holy relics entrusted to his care ... also the people who could escape from the castle rushed about in confusion ... After they had entered, the enemy thoroughly plundered the fortified city and the neighbouring *wik*; they made their appearance in the evening and remained that night and the following day and night. After completely ransacking the place and putting it to the flame, they disappeared again. The church, which had been rich in artistic objects, and the wonderful monastery erected by the bishop were burned to the ground. Together with numerous other books, the splendid bible given to our father by the noble emperor was destroyed. Everything which Ansgar possessed there, church vessels as well as other valuable objects, was lost, either robbed or burnt during the enemy's raid.

Even so, the collapse of the trade networks must have had even more dramatic consequences for all those who lived in these new centres.

[5] Edith Ennen, *The Medieval Town*, Amsterdam 1979, 49.

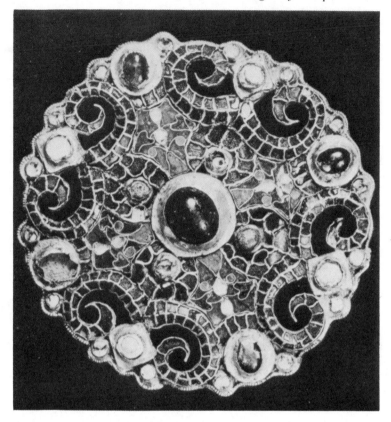

Fig. 64 A golden brooch found at Dorestad dating to Charlemagne's reign (Courtesy the Dutch State Archaeological Service)

To support the view that the 820s and 830s were crucial decades of change, we can now turn to the evidence from Dorestad. For some time the excavators of this entrepôt in the Rhine delta accepted the historical perspective that the emporium declined after many Viking raids from the later 830s to the 860s. These raids and the changing route of the Rhine itself were thought to be the reasons for the abandonment of this key centre in the 860s. The archaeology of Dorestad now suggests a different picture. In the first volume of excavation reports the excavators write as follows:

The numismatic evidence ... holds a strong indication that an important change in Dorestad's economic situation must have occurred around A.D. 830. At about that date, the regular influx of Carolingian coins, which had characterised the preceding period of at least fifty years, decreased considerably and the official Carolingian mint, which had been ... at Dorestad itself, stopped its issues ... it can hardly be doubted, however, that they reflect a decrease in Dorestad's prosperity and a waning of its trade relations.[6]

The archaeology, therefore, suggests that this particular emporium was in decline *before* the Viking raids, and was a substantially smaller community when the raiders actually arrived. If this is the case we must assume that it was also reflecting the changing economic aspirations of the Carolingians as their supplies of silver faltered and as internal political divisions led to civil war.

The civil war between the sons of Louis the Pious was not underestimated by contemporary historians, and we too must recognise its significance. Like the divisions within the caliphate, the civil war in Carolingia had a devastating impact upon the secular and ecclesiastical elites which had been fostering international trade. Hence it appears that the war of succession virtually terminated cross-Channel trade between the northern French courts and Hamwih, Saxon Southampton. The excavations at Southampton emphasise the point. There is plentiful evidence from Hamwih for a period of remarkable prosperity between about 790 and 820/830, when Wessex was under Mercian domination. With the rise of the local West Saxon dynasty under king Egbert, however, the port declined. This apparent paradox is only explicable in terms of political events across the Channel, and in some ways it may account for the bellicose policy of the West Saxons, who invaded Kent and Cornwall during Egbert's reign, thus establishing a polity that stretched from Land's End to Thanet. Once again, the famous raids on

[6] W.A. van Es & W.J.H. Verwers, *Excavations at Dorestad 1; The harbour: Hoogstraat 1*, Amersfoort 1980, 297.

Hamwih in 842 must have been made upon a settlement in decline.[7]

We cannot ignore this evidence or dismiss it simply as a coincidence. Nor can we wholeheartedly agree with Jan Dhondt, the historian of Quentovic, when he writes about the end of this great emporium: 'First of all we have to note the absence of deep roots in the case of these Merovingian mushroom towns. They do not seem solidly anchored to the soil. These emporia constituted alien enclaves within the Carolingian world rather than organically belonging to it.'[8] Mushroom towns they might have been, but they also played important roles in the Carolingian world. Indeed they are a reflection of Carolingian economic aspirations, and archaeology cautions us not to dismiss them as readily as contemporary chroniclers appear to have done simply because they were short-lived.

After 830

The civil wars in Carolingia shattered the last ten years of the Emperor Louis' reign. His death in 840 only served to exacerbate the divisions between his sons. These divisions were ultimately resolved in 843 after a series of campaigns when the three sons met at Verdun and there signed a treaty (Fig. 65). The result was that Charlemagne's legacy was apporioned between his three grandsons. Lothar, the eldest, held a corridor from Aachen to Italy. Louis the German, the next in line, held the territories to the east. Finally Charles the Bald, the youngest son by Judith, held western Francia. The invisible legacy of Charlemagne was slow to dissolve, but subsequently a unified state existed on only one occasion, for just three years after 884, when the son of Louis the German was briefly in command. After this it dissolved into a number of duchies and kingdoms resembling the patchwork of realms that had existed in Clovis' time. These territories rather than the Empire itself were to form the scaffolding of the Middle

[7] P. Lauer (ed.), *Nithard: histoire des fils de Louis le Pieux*, Paris 1964, 124; J.F. Cherry and Richard Hodges, 'The chronology of Hamwih, Saxon Southampton, reconsidered', *Antiquaries Journal* 58, 1978, 299-309.

[8] Cited by Ennen, op. cit., 45.

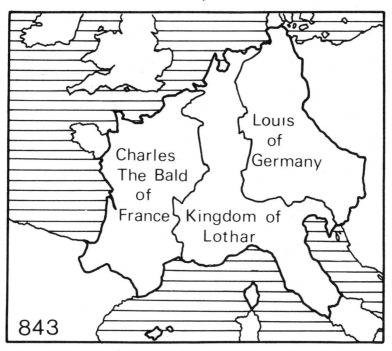

Fig. 65 The division of Charlemagne's empire at the Treaty of Verdun, 843

Ages. By contrast, the West Saxons built upon their steady gains made in the 820s and 830s under Egbert, and used these as the bases for a unified England in the early tenth century. King Alfred's achievement was founded against a background of the cessation of trade and the consequent need to readjust West Saxon economic policy during his grandfather's reign. His power, of course, came from his success in opposing the Vikings.

The Norsemen also reacted fiercely to the diminishing trade between east and west. Small-scale raids had been made on rich, undefended sites as early as 789 when Lindisfarne on Holy Island was sacked. But the number of raids intensified in the 830s and 840s with repeated attacks on Frisian, Flemish, East Anglian and West Saxon coastal sites.[9] It is difficult to determine the true scale of these onslaughts because the

[9] See Richard Hodges, *Dark Age Economics*, London 1982, ch. 8.

A   Anglo-Saxon

C   Carolingian

M   Arabic

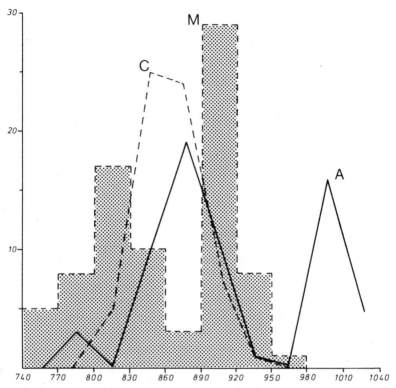

Fig. 66 A graph contrasting the discovery of Anglo-Saxon and Carolingian coins in the Baltic Sea contexts against those of Arabic dirhems. It illustrates the complementary character of the two sources of bullion, juxtaposing trade (with the Orient) and raids (on England and the Carolingian kingdoms). (After Klavs Randsborg)

archaeological evidence is slight and the monkish chroniclers – hardly dispassionate observers – were given to exaggeration. None the less the increasing references to the raids in the chronicles are borne out by the increase in coin-hoards buried in the fifty years after 835 (Fig. 66). In the 860s random pillaging turned to systematic invasion when the Danes began the annexation of the eastern English kingdoms. But king Alfred and the West Saxons blocked the Danish conquest of all the English kingdoms, and at the celebrated battle of Ethandun in 878 a partition of the country was agreed. Meanwhile the Seine valley was to come under persistent attack in the 890s. It was a threat that outlived the triumph of the Vikings in the British Isles, for in 911 Charles the Simple ceded a large part of northern France to the Norsemen. By this time Alfred's son, Edward the Elder, was campaigning in the Danelaw and annexing the area for the West Saxon dynasty.

At the very time that the Vikings were raiding Christian communities around the North Sea, Moslems from North Africa and Spain were also attacking Crete, Sicily, southern Italy, Provence and southern Anatolia. The raids began when the western Islamic kingdoms broke with the Abbasids in the 820s. The loss of wealth affected the political stability of the Maghreb and Umayyad Spain just as it had in the Baltic countries. Raids and invasions aimed at the vulnerable Christian communities were the result. In 827 a small

Fig. 67 A section of the Leonine Wall constructed by Pope Leo III. (Photo: Bryan Ward-Perkins)

renegade force landed in Crete and wrested control of the island from the Byzantines. In the same year, at the invitation of the discredited Byzantine admiral Euphemius, the Aghlabid amir of the Maghreb sent a large force to conquer Sicily. Palermo fell in 831, and gradually over the next seventy years the whole island was captured. After 830 raids on the Italian coast intensified. For more than twenty years, from 847 to 871, Bari, on the Italian mainland, was the capital of a small, independent, Islamic emirate. The sack of St Peter's, then outside the walls of Rome, in August 846, drew widescale condemnation, and a Carolingian offensive against the Arabs was launched, headed by the Emperor Lothar. It also led to the building of the Leonine wall (named after Pope Leo IV) around St Peter's (Fig. 67).[10] The Arab threat, however, was not easily removed, and until 915 it posed a constant threat to the Carolingians, Byzantines and smaller Christian kingdoms like Benevento. During this time centres like Naples and Salerno were repeatedly raided, and the great monasteries of Monte Cassino and San Vincenzo at Volturno were sacked and looted. Early in the tenth century, however, the raiders were confined to a single stronghold between Rome and Naples, and in 915 they were finally ousted altogether.[11] This success came as western Asia's trade with the Baltic and North Africa recommenced, and at the dawn of a Byzantine political revival. In fact, the removal of the Viking and Saracen threat symbolically marks the beginning of a commercial revival in the North Sea countries as well as in those around the Mediterranean. By this time, Charles the Great, to quote the chronicler Nithard, was 'a happy memory ... [who] ... left a unified Europe full of contentment'.[12]

---

[10] Sheila Gibson & Bryan Ward-Perkins, 'The surviving remains of the Leonine Wall', *Papers of the British School at Rome* 47, 1979, 30-57, and 51, 1983, 222-39.

[11] Nicola Cilento, *Italia Meridionale Longobarda*, Naples 1966, 175-89.

[12] Lauer, op. cit., 145.

8. Four Hypotheses

We have attempted to assemble the archaeological evidence relating to the debate about the thesis of Henri Pirenne. We must emphasise that our arguments are working hypotheses and that the only place they can be tested fully is in the field. Indeed there is an urgent need for extensive archaeological fieldwork in many parts of Europe. To take the isolated pockets of information and string them together to form a continuous historical narrative, as we have done, is hazardous. Nevertheless, with these reservations in mind, we conclude by formulating four hypotheses, which could – and should – be tested by archaeological research. In doing this we echo the brief conclusion of *Mohammed and Charlemagne*, which ends by formulating 'two essential points'.[1]

1.   The Roman social, political and economic systems did not collapse completely in the early fifth century; Mediterranean civilisation persisted until the sixth century. But between 400 and 600 there were massive and far-reaching developments, which led to the disintegration of the Mediterranean world. At present, the extent of these developments and the degree of disintegration is a matter of opinion. Nevertheless one simply cannot endorse Pirenne's view that the Mediterranean community in 600 was little different from that in 400. Indeed the archaeological evidence, such as it is, implies the contrary. By 600 the Western Empire was in the final stages of political and economic decay, and within the space of only one more generation the Eastern Empire too experienced a shift towards political and economic collapse. In other words, the transformation of the Mediterranean was well advanced before the first Arab incursion. By the time Carthage was besieged (in 698) the city

[1] Henri Pirenne, *Mohammed and Charlemagne*, London 1939, 284-5.

Fig. 68 Reverse of a Haithabu 'denier' imitating an eighth-century Frisian sceatta of wodan monster type, possibly minted at Dorestad. (Courtesy Kirsten Bendixen)

was a shadow of its former self, and its decay appears to be typical of cities, large and small, all over the Mediterranean. The creation of an Islamic empire in the later seventh and early eighth centuries was partly a product, not a cause, of the economic transformations detected by Pirenne. In sum, the archaeological evidence is beginning to endorse Anne Riising's critique of Pirenne's thesis some thirty years ago.[2]

2.   We cannot doubt that Pirenne was correct to emphasise the isolation of the Carolingians. We do question, however, whether – to use his emotive term – they were blockaded, and thus compelled to live upon their immediate resources. A more appropriate appraisal would be to recognise the disintegration of the Imperial state and to appreciate the nature of the political forces which replaced it. The archaeological evidence, when viewed in regional terms, suggests that early medieval Europe was governed by primitive political forces for whom market systems were

[2] Anne Riising, 'The fate of Henri Pirenne's thesis on the consequences of Islamic expansion', *Classica et Medievalia* 13, 1952, 87-130.

inappropriate. In anthropological terms, a world empire was replaced by a patchwork of chiefdoms or ranked societies, which in the seventh and eighth centuries formed fluid polities. The resources of the Rhine valley and its easy access to the North Sea in one direction and to South Germany in the other provided first the Austrasian and later the Carolingian kings with the means to expand their polity. Hence the axis of north-west Europe became once again aligned on the Rhine, as it had been before the Roman invasion.

3.   The archaeological evidence for rural settlements in the early medieval period is still too slight to tell us whether the Carolingians actually exploited their resources to fund the cultural renaissance of the early ninth century. This aspect of Pirenne's thesis must be tested, much as we have tested his perspective of Dark Age trade. Nevertheless it is clear that the Carolingians intensified craft production in the case of pottery, glass and querns. They appear to have achieved this by concentrating craftsmen at critical points within the kingdom (e.g. potters in the Vorgebirge Hills and quern-quarriers in the Eifel), just as the Romans had done.

In contrast to our meagre knowledge of rural settlement, we now possess a remarkable body of data on long-distance trade in the eighth and ninth centuries. A critical analysis of this shows that trade was directly controlled by kings and monasteries, and that its rationale was the movement of small quantities of prestige commodities and valuable raw materials.

The importance of trade to the Carolingian Renaissance seems to be beyond doubt. The commercial history of Dorestad mirrors the political rise and fall of the Carolingian dynasty. We argue that it was an important source of funds for the ambitious enlargement of churches and monasteries in the early ninth century. We have attempted to trace the source of these funds. The attempt took us back to a critique of *Mohammed and Charlemagne* which is almost fifty years old. Sture Bolin contended that in the early ninth century Charlemagne gained access to the large quantities of Abbasid silver imported to the Baltic region. By exchanging manufactured goods for silver, he argued, Charlemagne and later Louis obtained the wealth essential for developing the primitive Carolingian economy. We believe that the evidence of Dorestad and Haithabu, sharpened by dendrochronological dating, lends new credence to Bolin's imaginative hypothesis. Furthermore, we extend the argument to western Asia to illustrate that events in the Baltic and the North Sea can be

Fig. 69 A traditional seagoing sailing ship from Al-Hariri, *Maqamat* (Paris, Bibl. Nat. Ms. arabe 5847 fol. 119v), such as would have traded between Siraf and China. Painted in 1237, the illustration shows the stitched planking of the vessel

correlated – up to a point – with those in the Abbasid caliphate. Excavations at Siraf, for example, provide new evidence for the chronology and scale of Abbasid trade. A case exists, therefore, for regarding Abbasid silver as a significant additional source of wealth which, in conjunction with west Frankish trade to Anglo-Saxon England, and possibly with increased rural production, was essential for the consolidation of Charlemagne's massive empire.

4.   This brings us to a new dimension of the debate: why did Charlemagne want the silver? Indeed, in developmental rather than strictly historical terms, what is the meaning of the Carolingian Renaissance?[3] These are complex questions, and at this stage we can do no more than offer preliminary remarks which may help to explain this dramatic and important period in European history.

First, we must eliminate any belief that Charlemagne was brilliantly aware of the intricacies of the exchange networks linking Dorestad and Baghdad. On the other hand, his legislation makes it clear that he was aware of the need to consolidate his fragile administrative hold over his extensive empire. Evidently he appreciated that coinage might be used to articulate the regions of Carolingia and to generate sufficient taxation to finance a permanent military and administrative body. Whether he envisaged this as a gradual process or something which could be transacted overnight is a matter for speculation. In either case, monetary reform was of vital importance to his dynasty. In the short term the Church provided a powerful means of consolidating the Empire, which in theory was politically non-partisan. By increasing the prestige of the Church and revitalising its lacklustre spirituality, Charlemagne was able to use it to provide a ubiquitous and powerful force in the consolidation of his newly conquered territories. Hence he sought the Church's support to combat factions within the aristocracy. As a result, monasteries were favoured with considerable grants of land

---

[3] Walter Ullmann examines this question in: *The Carolingian Renaissance and the Idea of Kingship*, London 1969; see also Richard Hodges, *Dark Age Economics*, London 1982, ch. 10, for an alternative perspective of the issue.

Fig. 70 An unknown saint painted in the early ninth century. Found in the excavations at San Vincenzo at Volturno. (Photo: John Mitchell)

and moveable wealth, which enabled them to restore or enlarge their buildings. The prestige of the Church was thus quite evident, as was its close relationship with the

Carolingian court. This conspicuous spending on monuments to reinforce a vulnerable political system is a phenomenon found in many societies, both ancient and modern. In virtually all the cases discussed by archaeologists and anthropologists in recent years the fragile and short-lived hold of the kings results in large investments in prestigious monuments. The parallels with Carolingian Europe are striking. In this case, however, even a massive investment in the Church by the ruling family was insufficient to overcome the weakness of the political system. On top of this, the decline of long-distance trade in the 820s occurred at a disastrous moment for Louis the Pious. It may have been the catalyst of the social unrest – we do not know – but it was surely a significant factor in the civil wars of the 830s. The modest archaeological evidence for ninth-century rural settlement begins to suggest that monasteries were slow to develop their estates. Clearly they appreciated their task, as several surviving texts from the period show, but they lacked the necessary drive and administrative skill. Far from reinforcing the emperor's position, the lavish expenditure upon the Church served to exasperate the aristocracy.

By removing the critical role of Islam in the Mediterranean in the formation of early medieval Europe we have demolished one of the planks with which Pirenne constructed his historical model. As a result one might be tempted to dismiss Pirenne's thesis as a piece of interesting historiography. But we have little sympathy with the consensus view espoused by some historians, which deliberately under-emphasises the changes that came about in the period 400-850. The modern perspective is to place faith in gradual change rather than to identify the significant steps and processes involved in the emergence of medieval Europe. In a sense, historians have tended to believe what contemporaries tell us was the case rather than determining what actually happened from available sources. Archaeology provides a scale for these developments and makes us respect Pirenne's bold treatise.

We might therefore conclude that both Mohammed and Charlemagne were products of the collapse of Rome. That Islam was interested in the Roman Empire is improbable, but Charlemagne and his court were transfixed by the world of antiquity. We might, therefore, regard the creation and subsequent collapse of Charlemagne's empire as a vital force in the making of the Middle Ages. The ninth-century collapse, in particular, proved to be the catalyst to dramatic changes which have ultimately conditioned our world. In the shadow of Charlemagne the towns and villages of medieval Europe were founded and a new economic strategy was launched.

In the final analysis, archaeological evidence is becoming an increasingly important tool in the reconstruction of the Dark Ages. At the moment the absence of regional studies in France and Germany poses a serious obstacle, but one which is certain to be overcome. Archaeology, especially when dates are brought into sharp focus by the appreciation of dendrochronology, undoubtedly compels us to reconsider the historic period. Its essential quality is that 'it does not lie' (although we may misinterpret its evidence!), and when scientifically employed along the lines developed by modern theorists it has the potential to contribute significant insights into political systems as well as material culture. Henri Pirenne was a visionary, who might have appreciated these new strides towards a greater understanding of the past. For this reason, we end by echoing his biographer's sentiment:

Mahomet et Charlemagne ranks among the historical classics. It compels every scholar of the Middle Ages to wrestle with its concepts because within their framework rests a truer understanding and appreciation of the Middle Ages.[4]

---

[4] Bryce Lyon, 'A reply to Jan Dhondt's critique of Henri Pirenne', *Handelingen der Maat-schappij vor Geschiedenis en Oudheidkunde te Gent*, 29, 1975, 3-25, especially 23.

Index

Additional references

p. 44, n. 18: M. Gualtieri, M. Salvatore & A. Small (eds), *Lo scavo di S. Giovanni di Ruoti ed il Periodo Tardoantico in Basilicata*, Bari 1983

p. 46, n. 21: Richard Hodges, *A Dark Age Pompeii: San Vincenzo al Volturno*, London 1990

p. 74, n. 23: Paolo Delogu, 'The rebirth of Rome in the 8th and 9th centuries', in R. Hodges & B. Hobley (eds), *The Rebirth of Towns in the West, AD 700-1050*, London 1988, 32-42

p. 79, n. 2: Lotte Hedeager, 'Empire, frontier and the barbarian hinterland: Rome and northern Europe from AD 1-400', in M. Rowlands, M. Larsen & K. Kristiansen (eds), *Centre and Periphery in the Ancient World*, Cambridge 1987, 125-40

p. 85, n. 12: Alfons Zettler, *Die frühen Klosterbauten der Reichenau*, Sigmaringen 1988. Richard Hodges, *A Dark Age Pompeii: San Vincenzo al Volturno*, London 1990

p. 91, n. 14: Ulf Nasman, 'Vendel-period glass from Eketorp II, Oland, Sweden', *Acta Archaeologica* 55, 1984, 55-116

p. 100, n. 19: S. Lebecq, 'Dans l'europe du nord des VIIe-IXe siècles: commerce frison ou commerce franco-frison?', *Annales ESC*, 1986, 361-77

p. 105, n. 3: Alfons Zettler, *Die frühen Klosterbauten der Reichenau*, Sigmaringen 1988

p. 106, n. 4: Richard Hodges, *A Dark Age Pompeii: San Vincenzo al Volturno*, London 1990

p. 111, n. 9: Lene Frandsen & Stig Jensen, 'Pre-Viking and early Viking age Ribe', *Journal of Danish Archaeology* 6, 1987, 175-89

p. 125, n. 2: Thomas Noonan, 'The regional composition of ninth-century dirhem hoards from European Russia', *Numismatic Chronicle* 144, 1984, 153-65.

p. 173, n. 3: Richard Hodges, *A Dark Age Pompeii: San Vincenzo al Volturno*, London 1990